AMERICAN DYNASTIES

AMERICAN DYNASTIES

A History of Founding and Influential American Families

RACHEL DICKINSON

LYONS
PRESS

Essex, Connecticut

An imprint of Globe Pequot, the trade division of
The Rowman & Littlefield Publishing Group, Inc.
4501 Forbes Blvd., Ste. 200
Lanham, MD 20706
www.rowman.com

Distributed by NATIONAL BOOK NETWORK

British Library Cataloguing in Publication Information available

Library of Congress Cataloging-in-Publication Data available

ISBN 978-1-4930-4814-4 (cloth)
ISBN 978-1-4930-6669-8 (paperback)
ISBN 978-1-4930-4815-1 (e-book)

∞™ The paper used in this publication meets the minimum requirements of American National
Standard for Information Sciences—Permanence of Paper for Printed Library Materials, ANSI/
NISO Z39.48-1992.

Contents

Introduction

When most of us think of American dynasties, we imagine old white guys who have made their money in oil or banking or railroads, and then the succeeding generations. Many of the chapters that follow are about these very families, including the Rockefellers, the Astors, and the Morgans. I chose to look at these well-known captains of industry and finance and then follow the money for the next several generations. I was curious about what happens to families that inherit an unimaginable amount of wealth: Do they hang on to their wealth over the generations? Do family members try to increase that wealth, or do they just spend it? Do families have philanthropic impulses when faced with that amount of money? Does the wealth get diluted as more heirs come into the picture? What I found were combinations of all of the above.

I broadened my search for American dynasties beyond the obvious. Once I did that, I found more than Anglo American men. I found women (Maybelle Carter and her daughters and the Barrymores) and a family of Native American women (the Nampeyos). I found artists (the Wyeths) and brewers (Coors). I still wish there was more diversity within these pages.

What rings true for all of these dynasties is that the first generation always sets the tone. They are clever and hardworking and demand the same from others, whether they're family members or workers in a factory. Often, that second generation has a difficult time with the expectations of their elders, and this is when you find family members leaving or not engaging in the family business. The pressure in that second generation to succeed and carry on the work of their elders can be intense. Those that continue give rise to the third generation, and again you find some family members willing to soldier on in the family business, but many are content to spend the family money, either on philanthropic projects or on themselves.

It's important to remember that well into the twentieth century, the laws of inheritance always favored men, particularly the firstborn son. That's why very few women are profiled in these family stories. They are the wives and daughters who are in the background, and the family's hope for them is that they "marry well."

Rachel Dickinson

I

POWER

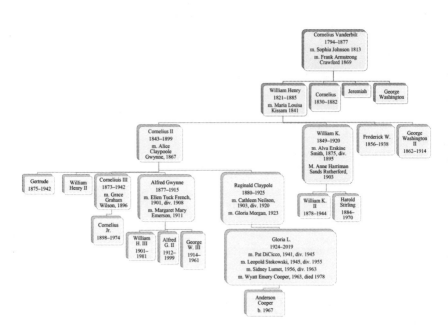

1

Vanderbilt

The Commodore's Legacy

Any fool can make a fortune; it takes a man of brains to hold onto it.
—CORNELIUS VANDERBILT

FOR OVER A CENTURY, THE VANDERBILT NAME HAS BEEN SYNONYMOUS with great wealth and upper-crust society in America. From Cornelius Vanderbilt to Gloria Vanderbilt, the nation's newspapers have tracked the ups and downs of the family with an almost prurient interest. And although, at the time, most would laugh at this pronouncement about a family of great wealth, it wasn't easy being a Vanderbilt.

CORNELIUS VANDERBILT
(1794–1877)

Cornelius Vanderbilt, the patriarch of the great family, was born on Staten Island, New York, into a hardworking family. Vanderbilt left school at age eleven to work with his father, who ferried cargo and passengers between Staten Island and Manhattan. Young Vanderbilt loved hard work and earning money. At age sixteen, he borrowed one hundred dollars from his mother to purchase a two-masted, flat-bottomed sailboat called a "perogue" (or periauger) that he used to start his own transport business. Vanderbilt was so

The patriarch. *Source:* Library of Congress.

3

hardworking and earnest that the other boat captains began calling him "The Commodore," a name that stuck for the rest of his life.

Vanderbilt married his first cousin, Sophia Johnson, at the age of nineteen, and they moved into a boarding house in Manhattan. Together they had thirteen children: Phebe, Ethelinda, Eliza, William, Emily, Sophia, Maria, Frances, Cornelius Jerimiah, George (who died at age four), Mary, Catherine, and another George.

In 1817 Vanderbilt became Thomas Gibbons's business manager. Gibbons ran a steamboat between New Jersey and New York. At that time, Gibbons was embroiled in a legal battle with Robert Livingston's heirs. Robert Livingston and Robert Fulton had been granted a monopoly to run steamboats between New York and New Jersey by the New York State Legislature. Aaron Ogden was running a ferry between New York and New Jersey on behalf of the Livingstons, and Gibbons was determined to put him out of business. Gibbons undercut his prices, and Ogden took Gibbons to court in the landmark case *Gibbons v. Ogden* that was ultimately decided by the Supreme Court. Gibbons sent Vanderbilt to Washington, D.C., to hire Daniel Webster to argue the case in front of the court. The Supreme Court justices ruled in Gibbons's favor, stating that States had no right to interfere with interstate commerce.

When Vanderbilt teamed up with Gibbons, the Vanderbilt family moved to New Brunswick, New Jersey, where Sophia Vanderbilt ran a very successful inn. Soon, Cornelius left Gibbons's employ and began to build up his own ferry lines, running boats in the Long Island Sound, in the lower Hudson River, and between New York and New Jersey. Daniel Drew ran one competing steamboat line. Vanderbilt and Drew teamed up to fight the Hudson River Steamboat Association that held a steamboat monopoly between New York City and Albany. In 1834 the Hudson River Steamboat Association paid Vanderbilt a lot of money to stop competing with them, at which point Vanderbilt switched his focus to the Long Island Sound.

Vanderbilt diversified his business interests in the 1840s. He bought real estate in Manhattan and Staten Island and took control of the Staten Island Ferry. Vanderbilt also saw the value of railroads, which were just coming to the region, in transporting cotton from the South to textile mills in the North. He gained control over small railroads connecting the Long Island Sound to New England. The prize would be the New York, Providence and Boston Railroad (known as the Stonington), which Vanderbilt took over after cutting the fares on competing lines, causing the value of the Stonington to plunge. Vanderbilt became president of this consolidated company in 1847.

In the 1840s, Vanderbilt built a large brick home for his family at 10 Washington Place, which is now in the Greenwich Village neighborhood. Even though he became the wealthiest man in America, he was never accepted by the city's elite. This was likely a reflection of his rough and uncultured manner. Although he had terrific business acumen, and kept all of his figures in his head, his lack of schooling reflected in his writing and his often loud and crude behavior. He also carried on numerous extramarital affairs.

When gold was found at Sutter's Mill in California in 1848, Vanderbilt, always looking for the next best thing, got into the ocean-going steamship business. In the days before the building of the Panama Canal, those traveling between the East Coast and the West Coast took a steamship to Panama, then crossed the isthmus by land. Vanderbilt wanted to build a canal across Nicaragua for two reasons: it was closer to the United States than Panama, and Vanderbilt could take advantage of two existing bodies of water, Lake Nicaragua and the San Juan River. He proposed building a canal to span the twelve miles between the lake and the Pacific Ocean but couldn't get the backing. Instead, he started a steamship line, Accessory Transit Company, from New York to Nicaragua, where passengers and freight would be transferred to boats across the lake and then taken overland to the Pacific Ocean to meet up with another Vanderbilt steamship. This was the cheapest route to California at the time.

As would be the case, time and again, Vanderbilt got into an argument with a partner in the Accessory Transit Company that escalated to the point where Vanderbilt put enough pressure on the company that his own company paid him off. Vanderbilt was ruthless in his business affairs and was not ever going to be taken for a fool. But this was not the end of his involvement with Accessory Transit. In 1855, William Walker, an American, led a coup in Nicaragua, taking over the government for some time (long enough that U.S. president Franklin Pierce recognized Walker's regime as the legitimate government of Nicaragua in May of 1856). Vanderbilt was furious that Walker was using Accessory Transit steamships to ferry supplies. He sent a secret agent to Costa Rica (all of the Central American republics were raising arms against Walker) to organize a raid to capture the steamboats on the San Juan River, cutting off Walker's supplies. The war ended, and Walker was thrown out of the country and sent back to the States. However, Vanderbilt never got back his transit business in Nicaragua, so he bypassed that country and started sending his steamships to Panama.

During the American Civil War, Vanderbilt's largest steamship, the *Vanderbilt*, was first leased and then donated to the Union Navy to help bolster the Union blockade at Hampton Roads, Virginia. After the war, Vanderbilt received a Congressional Gold Medal. Unfortunately, the war had a profound personal impact on Vanderbilt when his youngest and favorite son, George Washington Vanderbilt, enlisted, then fell ill and died before seeing combat.

Cornelius Vanderbilt spent the rest of his life in the railroad business. He sold all of his steamboats and concentrated, in particular, on the New York and Harlem Railroad, which was the only railroad to go into Manhattan. Vanderbilt placed his son William "Billy" as vice president of the Harlem, where he proved his mettle to the old man. Vanderbilt bought or fought for control of every railroad line that connected with the Harlem, eventually consolidating some of them into the behemoth New York Central and Hudson River Railroad. Vanderbilt built the Grand Central Depot on 42nd Street in Manhattan, now the site of Grand Central Terminal, and in a move that pleased those who lived in New York City, moved the tracks underground.

In a major dustup in 1868, now called the Erie Railroad War, Vanderbilt and Daniel Drew conspired against Gilded Age robber barons Jim Fisk and Jay Gould for financial control of the railroad. The newspapers had a heyday with the battle of the titans. Gould and Fisk gained ultimate control, but they had to pay Vanderbilt back for watered-down stocks they had issued during the fight for the Erie.

In that same year, Sophia Vanderbilt died. Cornelius married Frank Armstrong Crawford, a female cousin from Mobile, Alabama, who was forty years younger than the Commodore. 1n 1873, Vanderbilt gave $1 million to a relative of Frank's who wanted to start a university. Vanderbilt's donation both built and provided an endowment for Vanderbilt University in Nashville, Tennessee.

Cornelius Vanderbilt died at age eighty-two in 1877 at his home in Manhattan. Ninety-five percent of his fortune, estimated at more than $100 million at his death ($2.46 billion in 2020 dollars), was left to his son William and William's four sons. Each of his daughters received between $250,000 and $500,000. His wife, Frank, got the Manhattan house, stock in the New York Central Railroad, and $500,000. His other surviving son, Cornelius Jeremiah Vanderbilt, who was an alcoholic and gambler, was left the income from a $200,000 trust fund. He left nothing to charity. The will was challenged in court by two daughters and Cornelius. It was eventually settled out of court with William adding $500,000 to each sister's share and giving $400,000 more to Cornelius. But newspaper accounts of the trial had caused the Vanderbilts considerable embarrassment and social damage. In November 1877, the *Brooklyn Daily Eagle* reported the opening remarks by the injured parties' lawyer—that he intended to "proceed with the necessity of proving or disproving that Commodore Vanderbilt exposed his first wife to nameless ignominies at home and then drove her from that to nameless horrors in a mad house."

WILLIAM HENRY VANDERBILT
(1821–1885)

Any fool can make a fortune; it takes a man of brains to hold onto it
—The Commodore is said to have told his son William Henry "Billy" Vanderbilt, according to a family history written by cousin Arthur T. Vanderbilt II.

William Henry Vanderbilt, the Commodore's oldest son, always worked for his father. He was fifty-six when his father died and would, unfortunately, die a short seven years later. But in those years, he doubled the fortune his father left him, to almost $200 million.

It must not have been easy to be the heir apparent to the Vanderbilt fortune. William H. (to distinguish him from his son William K.) was very hands-on and, according to one historian, found it difficult to delegate work. But he knew all the ins and outs of the railroad empire that his father had spent years putting together.

William H. married Maria Louisa Kissam, who, like her husband, descended from Dutch and English families that settled in New York in the seventeenth century. Together they had nine children. Before his father died, William H. was recognized as the Commodore's heir and had earned a place of distinction in "aristocratic, fashionable circles." He collected art and was fond of the opera. At the time, he lent paintings to the new Metropolitan Museum of Art. He was one of the founders of the Metropolitan Opera House, which was built specifically to incorporate more boxes for the fabulously wealthy who paid $10,000 a piece for them.

Like his father, William H. was also passionate about horses. He was often seen driving his famous matched team, Aldine and Early Rose, along Fifth Avenue. His favorite horse was Maud S., known as "queen of the trotters." In 1883, while behind Maud S. and Aldine on a track, he drove a mile in a record two minutes and fifteen and a half seconds.

The railroads experienced explosive growth and turmoil during the 1870s and 1880s when William H. was the head of Vanderbilt's vast railroad network. At that time, railroad workers were underpaid for hazardous jobs (for example, a brakeman averaged about $1.25 a day for a twelve-hour day), and in 1877, the railroad owners called for a 10 percent cut in wages across the board. The workers went on strike, and, unlike other owners, Vanderbilt wisely kept the twelve thousand New York and Central workers employed by giving them $100,000 to split. He hoped this would mitigate the pay cut and told them he would rescind the cut "as soon as business improved to a point justifying such an advance."

The farmers hated the railroads because of exorbitant freight prices, and businessmen hated the railroads because of their practice of secretly giving certain favored shippers rebates on freight charges in the form of under-the-table payments. In 1879, the New York Legislature formed a committee to investigate the discounts. When William H. appeared before the committee, he denied that his railroads ever engaged in the practice. However, in the first six months of 1879, the New York Central had more than six thousand contracts with shippers involving rebates.

Trains were now incorporating sleeping, dining, and club cars. The Pennsylvania Railroad started an express train between New York and Chicago, cutting the running time from thirty-six to twenty-six hours. Vanderbilt felt forced to replicate this feat, and when asked if his limited service made money, he said that it did not and that he was forced to do this to keep up with the competition. Then he added, "The public be damned!" when asked if the limited provided a public benefit. This statement neatly summed up how the robber barons viewed their civic responsibility.

William H. doubled his father's inheritance by using financier J. P. Morgan to sell half of his railroad stock, which brought in $35 million and left the Vanderbilts still in control. He then plowed this money into U.S. government securities and bonds, which brought in another $54 million in returns.

In 1879, William H. and his two eldest sons, William K. and Cornelius II, began building grand mansions on upper Fifth Avenue in New York City as befitting their social status. William H.'s mansion was a double house with him, Maria Louisa, and their youngest son living on one side and his married daughters and Margaret residing on the other. It's hard for us to imagine the scale of these houses—William K.'s had a hundred rooms—built as showcases to the family's immense wealth. The houses had to be large enough to accommodate parties of up to five hundred people. William H. also filled his house with valuable European art he had been collecting for years. Today, none of these houses still stand.

William Henry Vanderbilt, the Vanderbilt patriarch for a short seven years, died suddenly on December 8, 1885. He was in a meeting in his study with Robert Garrett, president of the Baltimore and Ohio Railroad Company, when he suddenly leaned forward and dropped dead. He had made nine wills since his father died, fretting about burdening any of his offspring with too much money. He gave his two oldest sons, William K. and Cornelius II, $50 million each. Maria Louisa received the house and its contents, including the painting collection, and a gift of $500,000. The four daughters received the houses in which they lived. Each of the

William K. Vanderbilt Mansion. *Source:* Library of Congress.

children would receive the income of $5 million for life, and several of the grandchildren also received millions. He left $1.1 million as gifts to various charities.

Because William H. was only sixty-four when he died, his children were in their early forties or younger. This family had come into the largest inheritance in America, and everyone waited to see how they would spend it.

THE THIRD GENERATION AND OTHER VANDERBILT DESCENDANTS

Cornelius Vanderbilt II proved to be an excellent manager of the Vanderbilt railroad business. He leased the Boston and Albany Railroad from the State of Massachusetts for only $2 million, enabling the New York Central to reach most of the New England coast. Throughout his life, he contributed to many charities, including the YMCA. Cornelius II managed the railroads until his death in 1899, after which his brother William K. assumed the helm for a brief time before retiring to spend more time with his yachts and horses.

Cornelius II married Alice Gwynn in 1867 and, after her father-in-law's death, was referred to as Mrs. Vanderbilt, as the wife of the Head of the House of Vanderbilt. William K. married Alva Smith in 1875, and it galled her that she was always referred to as Mrs. William K. Vanderbilt. To Alva, being a society matron was extremely important. She gave a grand costumed ball in 1883. There were twelve hundred guests, and, according to the *New York World*, "$155,730 was spent on costumes, $11,000 on flowers, $4,000 for carriage hire, $4,000 for hair-dressing, and $62,270 for champagne, catering, music, and sundries." The Alice/Alva rivalry would move from New York City to the little beach town of Newport, Rhode Island, the premier American summer resort.

In 1885, Cornelius II and Alice bought a rambling seaside house in Newport called The Breakers, built less than a decade earlier for Pierre Lorillard, of the tobacco family. In 1892 the house caught fire and burned to the ground with no loss of life, but the loss of the furnishings totaled almost three-quarters of a million dollars.

When The Breakers burned down, William K. and Alva had nearly finished building the Marble House, designed by architect Richard

The Breakers. *Source:* Library of Congress.

Morris Hunt, which was meant to be the grandest house in Newport. It had fifty rooms—only one was designated a guest room—and many of the rooms were for the twenty-five live-in servants.

After The Breakers burned, Cornelius II and Alice also called in Richard Morris Hunt (who might reasonably be called the "family architect," having designed most of the Vanderbilt dwellings) to build on the site of The Breakers. Hunt designed a seventy-room house, with thirty rooms allotted to the servants. It was said that the Vanderbilts could give a dinner party for two hundred without calling in extra help. These two Vanderbilt houses represented the pinnacle of Gilded Age architectural extravagance in Newport, a town already known for upper-crust wealth. Add to these Vanderbilt homes the ten mansions on Fifth Avenue in Manhattan.

George Vanderbilt, the youngest son of William H., inherited his mother's mansion at 640 Fifth Avenue and William H.'s extensive art collection. George was twenty-three when his father died and had inherited $6,250,000, a pittance compared to his older brothers' $50 million each. He was philanthropic and gave land to Columbia University and also gave money to have a small public library built—designed by Richard Morris Hunt—that became part of the New York Public Library System. Like other members of the Vanderbilt family, George was interested in architecture and building but decided to look beyond Newport for the ideal site for his estate. He settled on Asheville, North Carolina, which he had visited with his mother in the 1880s. George began buying land near Asheville and, by the turn of the twentieth century, had acquired about one hundred thousand acres. It was here that George decided to build the largest private house in America.

In the late 1880s, Hunt began making sketches for Biltmore—the name of George's future estate in North Carolina—and he and his wife joined George Vanderbilt in Europe to visit stately homes in Britain and France and settled on the style of an early French Renaissance chateau. At 255 rooms, including a banquet hall at 72 feet long, 42 feet wide, and 75 feet high, Biltmore was enormous. A railway spur nearly three miles long had to be laid to bring the materials—mainly limestone from Indiana—to the building site from the main line. Hundreds of laborers were hired to work on the house, and a little town was constructed outside the front gates as worker housing. When completed, the house and grounds required a staff of eighty servants and several hundred groundsmen to work on the estate. Gifford Pinchot, friend of George and later the first chief of the U.S. Forest Service and then governor of Pennsylvania, came to Biltmore to manage the thousands of acres of forests surrounding the estate. Frederick Law Olmsted, the landscape designer of New York City's Central Park, agreed to design the grounds around the house. The sheer size and opulence of Biltmore, when finished, was unparalleled in America at the turn of the twentieth century.

The quietest of the Vanderbilt brothers in that third generation, Frederick, and his wife, Louise, built a fifty-four-room Palladian mansion perched on a cliff on the east side of the Hudson River in Hyde Park, New York, designed by McKim, Mead & White. This Hudson River beauty became the weekend getaway for Fred and Louise and was the site of opulent parties.

What these grandchildren of the Commodore set in motion was the shift from making a lot of money to spending it. The third generation was at the pinnacle of the social scene and spent their money to keep themselves there. Sailing yachts, luxurious oceangoing yachts, beautiful horses, fast cars, jewelry and dresses, and art and opulent mansions with servants and summer homes and winter homes—the Vanderbilts made themselves

Colonel Cornelius Vanderbilt III served in World War I. *Source:* Library of Congress.

the objects of desire by the hungry, tabloid-reading public. This era was also the beginning of Vanderbilt divorces that would titillate the nation for the next couple of generations. The yearning for status in Europe, as well as in America, produced marriages to titled peers in England.

Gertrude Vanderbilt, a member of the fourth generation, was a sculptor and an avid collector of American art. She married Harry Payne Whitney and used her money, her connections, and her private collection as the foundation for the Whitney Museum of American Art in Manhattan. Her brother, Alfred Gwynne Vanderbilt, best known, perhaps, for dying when a German U-boat torpedoed the *Lusitania*, spent his time trying to revive four-in-hand carriage driving.

Alfred Gwynne Vanderbilt died on the *Lusitania*. *Source:* Library of Congress.

The fourth generation also included Harold Vanderbilt, who was the director of the New York Central Railroad. But he is best known for defending America's Cup three times and, according to his obituary in the *New York Times*, as the "father of contract bridge—a game that in two decades spread to beguile 40 million people around the world."

Vanderbilt descendants—today they number about one thousand—have been engaged in a wide range of activities, including politics, business, science, and writing. John Hammond, the great record producer

Gertrude Vanderbilt Whitney, guardian of Gloria Vanderbilt. *Source:* Library of Congress.

who introduced the world to musicians like Bob Dylan, Bruce Springsteen, Pete Seeger, and Billie Holiday, was a great-great-grandson of the Commodore. Probably the best-known Vanderbilt in the twentieth century, a great-great-granddaughter of the Commodore, was Gloria Vanderbilt—fashion designer, artist, writer, memoirist, socialite, and businesswoman. The country was captivated by her custody trial in the 1930s that ended with Gloria becoming the ward of her aunt Gertrude Vanderbilt Whitney.

Gloria was married four times, including to conductor Leopold Stokowski, who was forty-two years her senior, and to director Sidney Lumet. According to her *New York Times* obituary written by Robert McFadden, she died at the age of ninety-five in 2019.

Five years before her death, Gloria Vanderbilt's son, CNN's Anderson Cooper (a sixth-generation Vanderbilt), told Howard Stern's radio show, "My mom's made clear to me that there's no trust fund." Generations of lavish spending by the Vanderbilt descendants depleted the Commodore's fortune—which by many calculations had made him the second-wealthiest person in the world—until it was gone.

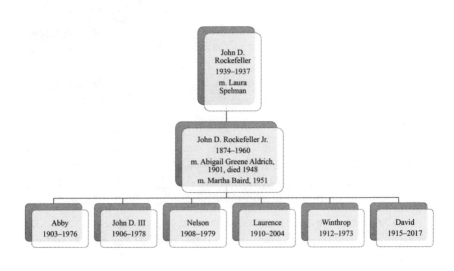

2

Rockefeller

Oil Titan

Mr. Rockefeller may have made himself the richest man in the world, but he has paid. Nothing but paying ever ploughs such lines in a man's face, ever sets his lips to such a melancholy angle.
—IDA TARBELL, WRITING ABOUT JOHN D. ROCKEFELLER

JOHN D. ROCKEFELLER (1839–1937) IS WIDELY CONSIDERED THE wealthiest American of all time and the richest person in modern history. He created Standard Oil, which became a behemoth corporation, in 1870. Through targeted philanthropy, he started foundations that had major impacts in medicine, education, and scientific research. The next two generations of Rockefellers included his son John D. Jr. and John Jr.'s six children, who became prominent philanthropists, bankers, conservationists, and politicians.

JOHN DAVISON ROCKEFELLER SR.
(1839–1937)
John Davison Rockefeller Sr. was born into a rough-and-tumble world in upstate New York in the 1830s. His father, William Avery Rockefeller, and Eliza Davison met when William, a traveling peddler of medicinal tonics, arrived at her family farm with a sign hanging around his neck saying he was "deaf and dumb." Eliza reportedly said, "If he wasn't deaf and dumb, I'd marry him." William could hear and speak, and in no time, he swept the young farmer's daughter into matrimony and then away, much to her father's dismay.

The young couple settled in an old farmhouse down the hill from Rockefeller's parents in Richford, New York. "Big Bill" or "Devil Bill," as

The patriarch, John D. Rockefeller Sr. *Source:* Library of Congress.

he was called, also brought his beautiful girlfriend, Nancy Brown, into the household as a "housekeeper." Over the next two years, Eliza and Nancy both had two children. Eliza's brothers finally interceded and made William move Nancy and her children out of the house.

Big Bill came and went, often leaving his family alone for months at a time. He would tell Eliza to buy things on credit and that he would settle when he returned, which he always did. One neighbor said, "I do not remember ever to have seen more pitiable neglected children. Their clothing was old and tattered, and they looked dirty and hungry." When John D. was three, the family moved to Moravia, New York. They were three miles from Eliza's family's farm, so Eliza had some support during her husband's long absences.

The Rockefeller family grew to five children as Big Bill continued his peripatetic ways. Where he went was a mystery, but he always came back, often driving a new team of horses and dressed in fancy new clothes. And he would bring back wads of cash. When they were still very young, Big Bill began doing business deals with his sons; "and I always cheat them to make them sharp," he said. He would lend them money at the prevailing interest rate and then call in the loans on a whim. These lessons would shape John D.'s business acumen. From his pious mother, John D. learned thrift, hard work, and self-control. Eliza and the children attended the local Baptist church each Sunday.

When John D. was ten, his father was accused of raping a housemaid, and Big Bill fled rather than face the charges. This incident was formative in young John D.'s developing self-reliance and a certain wariness of people who he assumed were always whispering about his father.

The Rockefellers still made several more moves in New York State before Big Bill moved them out to Cleveland, Ohio. It was here that John D. discovered that Big Bill was a bigamist and had married a second time under an assumed name. That was it for the teenaged John D., who spent the rest of his life trying—albeit unsuccessfully—to block Big Bill from his life. When his mother died, John D. told the preacher that she was a widow—although that was not true—perhaps as a way to dispose of his father once and for all.

John D. was a studious boy with hopes of attending college, but he dropped out of high school and got a job to help support his family. He found employment as an assistant bookkeeper and was an asset to the company from day one. The young Rockefeller had a real head for numbers and was thorough and exacting in perusing the bills. At this same time, John D. began keeping a personal ledger, something he would do for the rest of his life, as would his children. He recorded all purchases and contributions to charity throughout his life.

The young Rockefeller moved from bookkeeper to commodities trading—buying and selling grains and meat—with a friend. It was a risky venture, but Rockefeller was already a shrewd businessman at age eighteen. Then he caught wind of what was happening in northwest Pennsylvania, just across the state line. Oil had been successfully drilled for in Titusville, and much like in the gold rush of an earlier generation, men were flocking to the area to make their fortunes. John D. didn't want to get involved in the highly speculative drilling business but, rather, saw that the money was to be made in refining the oil into kerosene. Up to that point, Americans had relied on whale oil for lamp oil, but that was a finite commodity. Kerosene from oil would, in essence, bring American homes into the light. He borrowed thousands of dollars and built his first refinery right next to the train tracks that would bring the oil to Cleveland.

John D. also became very involved in his Baptist church in Cleveland. He volunteered, taught Sunday school, and always gave a percentage of his earnings to the church. He also gave to those he considered in need, including buying the freedom of a slave, giving to abolitionist causes, and funding orphanages. This philanthropic side of Rockefeller—this notion that he could do good in the world—would only grow stronger as he made more money.

In 1864, John D. married Laura "Cettie" Spelman. She had been valedictorian of her high school class, the same class John would have graduated from had he stayed in school. She seemed like a perfect mate for the hardworking young man. She was as devout as he was, and together they believed that John was doing God's work.

In 1870, the thirty-year-old Rockefeller created Standard Oil of Ohio, the very first company of the mammoth corporation that would change American business forever. In his effort to strengthen his own position in the oil business, he entered into a secret alliance—called the South Improvement Company—with the region's railroads. Rail freight rates were increasing. However, for Rockefeller and his allies, the rates were reduced for their regular shipments. Very soon, competitors of Rockefeller were either going out of business or selling to him. In a short two months, he was able buy out twenty-two of the twenty-six refineries in Cleveland. He was in the process of creating a vast monopoly of not only refineries but of everything having to do with the oil business. It was both horizontal and vertical integration. Standard Oil became a behemoth. By the time Rockefeller was forty, he controlled 90 percent of the oil refining in the world and soon would control 90 percent of the marketing of oil plus a third of all the oil wells.

Cettie and John D. moved to a mansion on "Millionaires Row" in Cleveland and got down to the business of raising their four children—Elizabeth, Alta, Edith, and John Jr. The Rockefellers lived modestly, which was quite a feat for America's richest man. The children shared toys and clothes and earned allowances for doing chores around the house. For

John D. and Cettie, it was all about building character. John Jr. and his sisters had to keep ledgers—just like their father—where they kept track of every penny earned and spent. They were to give to charity. When the children were adolescents, they had to sign oaths to abstain from using profanity, tobacco, and alcohol. Historian Albert Berger notes that Cettie was the disciplinarian and John D. was the cheerful, doting, indulgent father. The Rockefeller children were cut off from the outside world and hadn't any childhood companions outside of one another.

The Rockefellers moved to New York City in 1883. John D. moved the Standard Oil headquarters to 26 Broadway and set about creating the Standard Oil Trust. The trust was the umbrella corporation of the corporations that made up Standard Oil. Rockefeller reigned over an empire that seemed impenetrable to the outside world. By 1889, his fortune was more than $40 million. He hired a Baptist minister, Rev. Frederick Gates, to help him organize his philanthropic giving.

Gates pushed Rockefeller to give his money away faster than it grew. He funded Spelman College in Atlanta (a historically Black women's college), founded the University of Chicago, and supported public health and medical research. It was still not enough. Rockefeller worked so hard at both making and giving away money that he was making himself ill, so he took a month off to recuperate. In 1897, when he was fifty-eight, John D. retired from Standard Oil, but he kept the title of president because he was named, as president of Standard Oil, in several lawsuits.

In November 1902, *McClure's Magazine* began a nineteen-part series on John D. Rockefeller Sr. and Standard Oil Company. Written by Ida Tarbell, *McClure's* crackerjack investigative reporter, it would skewer the man and reveal the secret machinations of the corporation. Tarbell grew up in Titusville, Pennsylvania, and was no newcomer to the oil business. Her brother William Walter Tarbell was a founder of Pure Oil Company, a competitor of Standard Oil, and he sent Rockefeller enemies Ida's way as sources. Tarbell laid down a clear chronology and untangled the weeds of the convoluted oil industry. Tarbell just presented the facts for the readers and allowed them to seethe and simmer over the lack of fair play. She bemoaned the loss of competition in the marketplace. Tarbell went after Rockefeller, writing, "Mr. Rockefeller has systematically played with loaded dice, and it is doubtful if there has ever been a time since 1872 when he has run a race with a competitor and started fair."

There was silence from Standard Oil as the series cranked on. The only thing that made John D. furious was when Ida Tarbell ended her series with a character study of him. John D. had refused to meet with Tarbell, so she and her research assistant surreptitiously observed him while he was at church. Rockefeller had been suffering from alopecia for several years and did not appear in public outside of church because he was so self-conscious of the hair loss. Tarbell wrote in part:

> *The disease which in the last three or four years has swept Mr. Rockefeller's head bare of hair, stripped away even eyelashes and eyebrows, has revealed all the strength of his great head . . . the big cheeks are puffy, bulging unpleasantly under the eyes, and the skin which covers them has a curiously unhealthy pallor. It is this puffiness, this unclean flesh, which repels, as the thin slit of a mouth terrifies. . . . Mr. Rockefeller may have made himself the richest man in the world, but he has paid. Nothing but paying ever ploughs such lines in a man's face, ever sets his lips to such a melancholy angle.*

The Tarbell articles really took a toll on the Rockefeller family. John D. Sr. had serious stomach ailments, Cettie was ill and bedridden, and John D. Jr. spent every evening with a migraine headache.

At the same time the *McClure's* series was running, John D. Jr. began building a house for his parents at his immense estate at Pocantico Hills on the east side of the Hudson River. After a few false starts, Kykuit emerged, surrounded by sumptuous landscaping, gardens, and a golf course. Kykuit would prove to be a retreat from the world for the Rockefellers, who kept intruders away with Pinkerton guards. On May 15, 1911, the U.S. Supreme Court declared that Standard Oil was a monopoly in restraint of trade in violation of the Sherman Antitrust Act and should be dissolved. The Rockefellers heard the news from behind the closed gates of the estate. Congress then strengthened antitrust laws by passing the Federal Trade Commission Act and Clayton Antitrust Act.

Rockefeller didn't mind busting the trust, for he rightly saw that the individual companies would be worth more than the large corporation. After a few years, Rockefeller had accumulated the greatest personal fortune in history—a fortune equivalent to $280 billion in today's dollars, which at that time was the same as nearly 2 percent of the American economy.

The billionaire Rockefeller spent the rest of his life giving his money away—to his children, to his church, and to his philanthropies, among them the University of Chicago, the Rockefeller Foundation, the Rockefeller Institute for Medical Research (now known as Rockefeller University), and the Rockefeller Sanitary Commission. His largesse worked to eliminate hookworm, malaria, scarlet fever, yellow fever, tuberculosis, and typhus. He established the first school of public health and hygiene at Johns Hopkins University in 1918 and created public health programs at universities around the world. In 1909, he donated $50 million to establish the Rockefeller Foundation, whose mission was "to promote the well-being of mankind throughout the world." For decades, the Rockefeller Foundation distributed more foreign aid than the entire U.S. government, according to the Philanthropy Roundtable, which tracks this information.

John D. Rockefeller Sr. often said he had two goals in life: to be a rich man and to live to one hundred. He succeeded in the first and just missed the second. He died at the age of ninety-eight in 1937. For the last almost twenty years of his life, after the death of Cettie in 1915, he enjoyed more of a social life. He golfed on his estate right up until the year he died. He began to like publicity, particularly if it meant being on newsreels. And he loved the company of his grandchildren. He also began the habit of carrying a pocketful of dimes, which he would hand to adults, and a pocketful of nickels, which he would hand to children. He didn't like signing autographs, so this became a handy substitute. Ruthless in business but kind in his personal life, John D. Rockefeller Sr. should be best remembered as a complicated person.

JOHN D. ROCKEFELLER JR.
(1874–1960)

The only son of the richest man in the world felt the immense burden of wealth weighing on his shoulders for his entire life. Whereas his father was a self-made man, John D. Jr. was born into extreme wealth, and he spent his life trying to do something good with his fortune. One of the most important lessons Cettie taught her children was "What is your duty?"—you have a purpose beyond your own enjoyment. By the age of eighteen, John D. Jr. had already suffered two nervous collapses.

Young Rockefeller entered Brown University in 1893, and soon he met Abby Aldrich, a Providence girl and daughter of Nelson Aldrich, a United States senator from Rhode Island. She was not put off by John D. Jr.'s name and pedigree, which was a relief

John D. Rockefeller Jr., the only son of the billionaire father. *Source:* Library of Congress.

to the young man. When Rockefeller graduated from Brown, he went to work for Standard Oil. He reported to 26 Broadway, and when he got there, nobody knew what he was supposed to do, although he had a desk and was drawing a salary. John D. Sr. told his son to relax and learn the business. At the same time, John D. Jr. was courting Abby, and it took four years for him to get up the nerve to ask her to marry him. His mother finally pushed him to ask her, culminating in a wedding that was the picture of Gilded Age opulence.

As his father and company endured the backlash of Ida Tarbell's articles, John D. Jr. took it upon himself to build a new home for the elder Rockefellers. According to historian Judith Sealander, "Ida Tarbell really took a toll on the family. John Jr. certainly had what could only be described as a really catastrophic nervous breakdown." At the same time, John and Abby's family began to grow. First came Abby "Babs," then John D. Rockefeller III, then Nelson, Laurance, Winthrop, and David. When John D. III was born, newspapers called him the "Richest Baby in History."

In 1910, at the age of thirty-six, John D. Jr. withdrew from Standard Oil and decided to help with his father's philanthropic ventures. He and his father launched the Rockefeller Foundation with the goal to "promote the well-being of mankind throughout the world." Unfortunately, the elder Rockefeller's businesses were not done testing young Rockefeller, who held on to stock in one Standard Oil company—Colorado Fuel and Iron—where he owned a controlling interest and sat on the board.

In 1913, eight thousand miners decided to strike at Colorado Fuel and Iron, demanding humane living and working conditions. The company immediately evicted workers and their families from their company-owned homes, and the striking miners lived in a tent community in Ludlow, just beyond company grounds. It was fall. It was getting cold. And twenty thousand men, women, and children suffered as the strike dragged into the snowy Colorado winter. Union organizers, including Mother Jones, landed in Colorado, trying to rally the strikers. The strike dragged on into the spring of 1914, and John D. Jr. was called to testify before Congress as a company director. He told the congressional committee that he trusted the company managers and that he also believed in an open shop. Two weeks later, thirty-five National Guardsmen perched on a hill above the tent colony in Ludlow. A shot rang out—no one is really sure from where—and the guardsmen began raking the tent colony with machine-gun fire. Soon the tent colony was engulfed in flames, and the next morning, the bodies of two women and eleven children were discovered in a bunker beneath one of the tents. The death toll stood at twenty-four, with many more injured and burned.

John D. Jr. was vilified in the press. Upton Sinclair publicly called him a murderer. An angry mob threatened to storm the gates of Kykuit. The striking workers had to return to the mines in December 1914 when their relief funds were exhausted. Young Rockefeller was again summoned to testify before a government commission investigating the strike, where he then admitted that he had been wrong. He promised to go to Ludlow to speak to the miners.

In 1915, when he arrived in Ludlow, Rockefeller was horrified by what he saw. The miners and their families lived in tent cities with no potable drinking water. The conditions were squalid, and their children were thin. The normally shy Rockefeller knew he had to speak up. He promised the miners that they would not be fired if they chose to join a union, but he also offered his own plan to address worker grievances. In a secret ballot, the miners voted for the Rockefeller plan.

After watching his skillful negotiations in Colorado, John D. Sr. began to transfer his wealth to his son. The events in Ludlow were the beginning of John D. Jr. trying to recast the Rockefeller name from being synonymous with robber baron to being that of philanthropic benefactor.

John D. Jr. spent the rest of his life trying to do good. He threw himself into projects he cared about—medicine, science, education, the arts, foreign policy. His pet projects included restoring the palace at Versailles, saving the giant redwoods in California, buying land and giving it to the government to create the Grand Teton National Park, and building a medical college in China. He was everywhere, and that took a toll on his health. He suffered from debilitating migraines, and in 1922 he took a rest cure at Dr. Kellogg's Battle Creek Sanitarium in Michigan.

Abby Aldrich Rockefeller became fascinated with modern art and was a founding member of the Museum of Modern Art. John D. Jr. indulged her but didn't understand her fascination with art that he didn't like. His son John D. III would tellingly say, "Father always has his own way. He is so wonderfully broad in business relations but so narrow in some of his family details."

John D. Jr.'s interest in art was realized in the building of The Cloisters, where he created a kind of medieval retreat that he could fill with his art treasures. He also spent $55 million to restore the colonial capital of Williamsburg, Virginia, to his sanitized version of the past. Whereas Abby looked to the future and was fascinated with where art was going, her husband idolized and idealized the past.

In the late 1920s, the Metropolitan Opera was looking for a new home, so John D. Jr. bought three blocks of properties right before the stock market crash of 1929 plunged the country into the Great Depression, which wiped out half of the Rockefeller fortune. Rockefeller developed shingles and colds he couldn't shake. Instead of building a new opera house, Rockefeller decided to concentrate on commercial buildings, which resulted in the seventy-story tower, Rockefeller Center, surrounded by thirteen buildings. During the Great Depression, Rockefeller employed 75,000 workers to create his vision. He hired his son Nelson to handle the rentals and public relations. Nelson, in consultation with Abby, hired the Mexican muralist Diego Rivera to paint a mural called *Man at the Crossroads Looking Hopefully toward the Future*. The huge fresco, 63 feet long and 17 feet high, was vivid and bright, but there was a problem. Rivera painted the head of Lenin into the fresco and refused to remove it when Nelson said it had to go. Rivera was paid in full, and the fresco was destroyed. In 1939, as Rockefeller Center neared completion, sixty-five-year-old John D. Rockefeller Jr. could look back on his life and be satisfied with his achievements.

THE THIRD GENERATION

The children of John D. Jr. felt they had a lot to rebel against. The old-est—Abby "Babs"—wanted to be out from under the strictness of the Rockefeller household. She escaped by marrying at age nineteen. The boys took a different, slightly less confrontational tack in their attempt to act like modern teenagers. They did not openly confront their father and tried to keep him ignorant of any activities he might have found unacceptable. They engaged in a "constant subterranean rebellion," said historian Peter Collier.

The five boys would all make their mark and really come of age during World War II. When they came back from the war, they descended on Rockefeller Center and took up offices in the RCA building. Nelson was always considered the one who would go places—he was outgoing and personable and had high political aspirations. John III was shy and happy to be out of the limelight running the family philanthropies. He became very interested in population control and U.S.-Asia relations. Laurance invested in aviation and new technologies and built resorts in the tropics with an eye toward conservation. David rose through the ranks at Chase Bank and championed urban renewal. Winthrop, the odd man out when they were children, went to Arkansas, bought a cattle ranch, and eventually became governor of Arkansas. And after her father's death, even Babs became involved in a philanthropic cause, supporting the Sloan Kettering Cancer Center.

According to historian Peter Collier, "If there was an establishment in America in the 1950s, it was these Rockefeller brothers. These young men have taken their place as these absolutely unique members of a unique family. They're in some sense, the very tip of this kind of the American century, the American experience, this optimism that buoys America, in the post-war era."

In 1958, Nelson Rockefeller ran for governor of New York State and won. John D. Jr.'s grandson Steven Rockefeller said, "The fact that Nelson had been elected was a sign to [John D. Jr.] that the people of the United States had in fact, fully accepted the Rockefellers in spite of the early history of the family." John D. Jr. died two years later in 1960 at the age of eighty-six and was regarded as one of the world's foremost philanthropists, having given away over half a billion dollars in his lifetime.

Nelson Rockefeller campaigning in New York City. *Source:* Library of Congress.

In 1961 Nelson moved his family into Kykuit and then announced that he and his wife Mary Tod Clark were divorcing after thirty years of marriage. Two days later, they were told that their son Michael was missing in Papua New Guinea. The twenty-three-year-old was on a scientific expedition when he disappeared. Nelson, and Michael's twin, Mary, went to New Guinea to search for him, but Michael was never found. Nelson Rockefeller was reelected governor of New York the following year in a landslide. There was talk of running for president in 1964.

Rockefeller held a sizable lead coming up to the Republican primaries of 1964. Then, Nelson married Happy Murphy, a divorced woman who had four young children. In the early 1960s, that was not going to sit well with the voters. He lost the nomination to conservative Barry Goldwater.

Still the governor of New York, Rockefeller created the State of New York University system and engaged in a massive building project creating a new capitol building and what is now known as the Nelson A. Rockefeller Empire State Plaza. He opened fifty new state parks, fixed miles of highway, and built hundreds of water treatment plants. Although Nelson Rockefeller would never be president, he served as Gerald Ford's vice president in the mid-1970s.

A significant black spot, at least to the next generation of liberal Rockefellers, was Nelson Rockefeller's 1971 decision to send one thousand state troopers to quell a prison riot at Attica State Prison in the western part of New York State. The inmates wanted better living conditions and amnesty for the takeover. They held forty-two prison guards hostage. After five days, Rockefeller ordered the state police to act. In less than six minutes, twenty-nine inmates and ten hostages were killed as the inmates and troopers exchanged gunfire. Historian Peter Collier said, "In these times when Marxism was taken seriously in America, [the Rockefellers] were seen as the loadstone, the Rosetta stone. It's 'find the Rockefellers, and you understand power in America and how it works.'"

As that generation of Rockefeller descendants died—first Winthrop, then John III and Nelson—"the cousins" (the next generation) were called to step up and do good works with the massive family fortune accumulated over the generations. Today, that fortune is estimated at $11 billion, and they are no longer the richest family in America. And, according to a recent *Forbes* article, "The Rockefeller clan is as secretive as it is influential, and the majority of the family manages to skirt the public eye." But this family, now in its seventh generation, continues to hew close to the founder of the family by thriving in business, political, and philanthropic spheres.

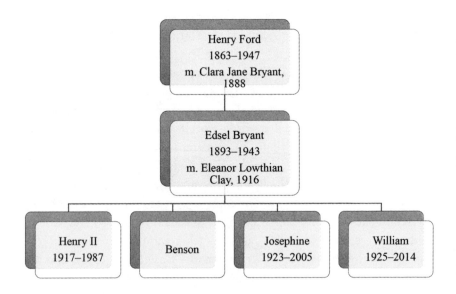

3

Ford

Putting Wheels on the Modern Age

I'm going to start up a museum and give people a true picture of the development of the country. That's the only history that's worth preserving.

—HENRY FORD

PERHAPS NO AMERICAN FAMILY HAS HAD A MORE SIGNIFICANT IMPACT on consumer culture, transportation, mechanization, industrial workers, and philanthropy than the Ford family.

HENRY FORD
(1863–1947)

Henry Ford was born on a farm outside of Dearborn, Michigan, to William Ford (an Irish immigrant) and Mary Litogot (the child of Belgian immigrants). The oldest of four siblings, it was expected that he would take over the family farm, but he had no interest in farmwork. His father gave him a pocket watch when Henry was twelve, which he took apart and put back together. He had a gift for mechanical tinkering. Soon, he had a business repairing his neighbors' watches.

His mother died in 1876 when Henry was thirteen, devastating the boy. Ford left home three years later to work as an apprentice machinist in Detroit. He returned to Dearborn in 1882 when he was nineteen to work on the family farm. Fortunately, there was a Westinghouse portable steam engine there for him to work on and master. Soon he became Westinghouse's representative in the region, traveling to other farms when they had trouble with their machines. While on the farm, Ford built three cars

Josephus Daniels—journalist and Secretary of the Navy during World War I and Ambassador to Mexico—and the patriarch Henry Ford (on the right). *Source:* Library of Congress.

in his own workshop, first using steam, which he found unsuitable for light vehicles, then using gasoline.

In 1888, Henry Ford married Clara Jane Bryant. Their only child, Edsel, was born in 1893. By this time, Ford, who had joined the Edison Illuminating Company in Detroit as an engineer a couple of years earlier, was promoted to chief engineer. He now had enough time and money to work on his gasoline engines. In 1896, he completed the Ford Quadricycle.

Within half a dozen years, Ford had founded and dissolved the Detroit Automobile Company, built and raced a 26-horsepower automobile, and built an 80-plus-horsepower racer, "999," which Barney Oldfield raced in 1902 and then took around the country promoting the Ford name.

The Ford Motor Company was founded in 1903 with $28,000 in capital. By 1908, it introduced the Model T. The car was simple to drive and cheap to repair. The steering wheel was on the left—soon to be the industry standard. The original cost of $825 in 1908 dropped throughout the decade. Half of all cars in America were Model Ts, making it the car of the "everyman." All Model Ts were painted black because of the paint's quicker drying time. By 1914 sales passed 250,000, and two years later, the price dropped to $360, and Model T sales were at almost half a million. By the end of its run in 1927, the Ford Motor Company had sold over 15 million Model Ts.

Henry Ford preached the social virtues of dependable, inexpensive vehicles. Early in his career, he told his colleagues, "There are a lot more poor people than wealthy people. We'll just build one car for the poor people." To build cars quickly, Ford hired people to help him streamline the production, leading to the first assembly line. In this manufacturing

Ford Motor Company assembly line at the Highland Plant. *Source:* Library of Congress.

model, the "car" came to each worker's station; the worker then did his one job (for example, tightening a bolt that had been put in place by the worker ahead of him), and then the car moved down the line. This kind of work was mind-numbing and repetitive for the workers, but the Ford Motor Company was able to radically speed up the process of assembly, pushing many more automobiles into the hands of an eager car-buying public.

In 1914, Ford doubled the standard wage of automobile workers to $5 per day, and he shortened the workday to eight hours. At that point, the company had 26,000 employees, and this move to a higher wage cost the company more than $10 million. Henry Ford said, "We believe in making 20,000 men prosperous and contented rather than follow the plan of making a few slave drivers in our establishment millionaires." This populist move also ensured that the Ford Motor Company would have people who could afford to buy their cars.

During World War I, Henry Ford was an antiwar activist. He believed that war was a terrible waste of human life, hindered long-term economic growth, and profited a minority of businesses. He blamed Wall Street bankers and financiers for dragging the United States into the war. In 1915 he gathered other peace activists, and together they sailed in what was dubbed the "Peace Ship" to Norway, a neutral country, with the aim of sponsoring a giant peace conference in Oslo. It was a total fiasco from start to finish, and Ford was roundly ridiculed in the press for promoting the idea. The final straw was when influenza swept through the ship, and many caught pneumonia, resulting in one death. Ford holed up in his Oslo hotel when the ship docked and headed back to the States as quickly as possible.

He fully supported President Woodrow Wilson, and once Wilson accepted the inevitability of American participation in World War I, the Ford Motor Company worked exclusively for the government from April 1917 to November 1918. Wilson urged Ford to run for the U.S. Senate in 1918—which he did—but he did not campaign for the seat. He viewed himself as a citizen candidate and appealed to the public as an honest reformer. He lost by only 2,400 votes.

The 1920s was the Age of Ford. Ford's innovations were vital in creating the new consumer culture. Cheap cars and creative marketing appealed directly to a buying public that wished to be seen as modern. He loved nature and was unusually modest. He exemplified the ethic of public virtue by building a hospital in Detroit in 1914. Ford became one of the most famous men in the United States. He kept himself in tip-top physical shape—he liked to run and walk—and he joined his friends Thomas Edison, Harvey Firestone, and John Burroughs on rustic camping outings. Known as the "Four Vagabonds," they all loved bird watching and nature. And the resulting publicity wasn't bad for any of them, either.

In 1919, Henry Ford sued the *Chicago Tribune* for libel over an editorial in 1916 that denounced Ford as an "ignorant idealist ... and an anarchistic enemy of the nation." The *Tribune* attorneys claimed that Ford's pacifist campaign had weakened the military preparedness of the American government and that he deserved the label *anarchist*. The defense called Henry Ford to the stand, where he proceeded to make a fool of himself. He proved to be ignorant in basic history (didn't know when the American Revolution started), and he said he was not a fast reader and didn't mind giving the impression that he was illiterate. *The Nation* wrote: "The mystery is finally dispelled. Henry Ford is a Yankee mechanic, pure and simple, quite uneducated, with a mind unable to bite into any proposition outside of his automobile and tractor business. . . . He has achieved wealth but not greatness." But the common man rushed to his defense. He was the everyman. "Ford comes nearer being typical of the average, energetic, courageous, uncultured American than any other one man in this country," wrote one small-town paper. He became the most quoted citizen in the United States.

By 1920, the Ford Motor Company had built an enormous plant on the River Rouge in Michigan. Ford hoped to produce ten thousand vehicles per day in this plant, which was possible by controlling the production process from beginning to end. Called "vertical integration" by the experts, River Rouge had its own power plant, a coke furnace where the steel was made, a sawmill and a foundry on site, and a massive building that held the assembly line. As Ford told one of his managers, he "wanted the raw materials coming in on one end of the Rouge plant and the finished cars going out the other end." In a *New York Times* article from 1925, author Evans Clark concluded that the Ford Motor Company "is probably the most completely integrated industry in the country if not the world . . . integration was completely realized in the Rouge, which stood as one vast interlocking self-improvement organization" where "undreamed of standardization becomes possible." Henry Ford had absolute control over the largest manufacturing enterprise in the world. This made him incredibly wealthy; yet, despite his wealth, he remained a hero to ordinary citizens.

There were some troubling aspects to Henry Ford's behavior. In 1919, he began publication of the *Dearborn Independent*. This newspaper carried no advertisements, and he made all of the Ford dealerships carry multiple subscriptions to the paper. Between 1919 and 1928, there were anywhere from 250,000 to 500,000 subscribers. A ghostwriter produced editorials under Ford's name. In 1920 the paper began a controversial weekly series titled "The International Jew: The World's Problem" that ran for over two years. The articles were filled with stereotypes and slurs, and the blatant anti-Semitism caused an uproar. Although Ford repudiated these articles in the late 1920s, the specter of his anti-Semitism would follow him for the rest of his life.

In 1938, Henry Ford accepted an award—The Order of the Grand Cross of the German Eagle—from the government of Adolf Hitler, the highest honor given to a foreigner by the Reich. Henry Ford became the first American citizen to be decorated with this award.

Through the 1920s, the Ford Motor Company's share of the automobile market began to slide. Rather than produce cars that the changing tastes of consumers demanded, Henry Ford stubbornly hung on to production of the Model T. In late 1926, however, Henry Ford approved the design of a new four-cylinder auto to replace the Model T, giving birth to the Model A. The plant had to close for six months to retool for the new car, which cost the company $250 million. Costing no more than the Model T, the new cars were lightweight, with a four-cylinder, forty-horsepower engine that could reach cruising speeds of sixty-five miles per hour. They had sleek bodylines, safety glass, hydraulic shock absorbers, an automatic starter, windshield wipers, and theft-proof locks. And better yet, these cars came in a variety of colors.

On October 21, 1929, Henry Ford brought Thomas Edison to Dearborn to commemorate the fiftieth anniversary of the incandescent lamp. He called it Light's Golden Jubilee. Ford had taken apart then reconstructed Edison's laboratory, library, and machine shop from Menlo Park, New Jersey, overwhelming Edison with the careful restoration and attention to detail. The Menlo Park reconstruction was part of an American village—Greenfield Village—being built to hold houses, farms, machine shops, and public buildings from the eighteenth and nineteenth centuries. Ford was creating a sentimentalized vision of America at an earlier age. This is what Henry Ford saw as "the real history." He would scour the countryside and buy up buildings that were then dismantled, brought to the village, and reconstructed on site. By the late 1930s, there were almost one hundred buildings in Greenfield Village, including Stephen Foster's house and the Wright Brothers bicycle shop (where they had built the first plane).

Ford also created the Ford Museum—which he referred to as "his Smithsonian Institute"—filled with everyday objects from the past. "I'm going to start up a museum and give people a true picture of the development of the country. That's the only history that's worth preserving,"

A room in Thomas Edison's Menlo Park Lab after it was brought to Ford's Greenfield Village. *Source:* Library of Congress.

he said. By the 1930s, Henry Ford was spending most of his time in the museum or at the village rather than at his plant. His version of history focused on ordinary people and their daily lives and not on politicians and wars and great events. He embraced a populist sense of history, a history of progress where nativism was coupled with nostalgia.

As America grappled with the Great Depression, from 1931 to 1933 the Ford Motor Company lost $140 million and slid to the number-three spot, behind General Motors and Chrysler. Ford did not like President Franklin D. Roosevelt and denounced the New Deal, which Ford believed violated fundamental American values. Things had changed in the Ford Motor Company plants. In 1916, Ford had hired Harry Bennett, who rose to be the head of security.

Bennett became Ford's chief labor negotiator during the Depression in Ford's attempt to thwart unionization. The workers were pushing against deplorable conditions at the Ford factories, where there were fewer workers doing more work in less time. They weren't allowed to talk during their shift and were allowed only a fifteen-minute lunch break. By 1941, the Ford Motor Company still did not recognize the UAW (United Auto Workers), even after the workers held a massive strike at the Rouge plant. The workers held a union vote to work with the AFL/CIO, but Ford refused to sign the contract the union drafted. Finally, Ford's wife, Clara, threatened to leave him if Ford did not sign the contract.

From around 1914 until his death in 1947, Henry Ford maintained an extramarital relationship with Eve Cote Dahlinger, a woman who worked for the Ford Motor Company and was thirty years his junior. She had a son, John, in 1923 who was rumored to be the son of Henry Ford. Ford lavished gifts upon John throughout the boy's childhood. Henry Ford and Eve Dahlinger neither confirmed nor denied the rumor. Eve had a rocky marriage with Henry Ford's chauffeur, Ray Dahlinger, and the two of them, plus John, lived in a Tudor-style mansion not far from Fair Lawn, the Ford estate. When Ford was on his deathbed in 1947, Clara Ford telephoned Eve asking her to come over to the house to see Henry one last time.

During the last four years of his life, Henry Ford became increasingly more confused. The death of his only son Edsel in 1943 pushed him into an emotional nosedive from which he never recovered. In 1945, Ford's physician said, in a deposition, that Ford "had no recollection . . . and became limited to 'yes' and 'no' answers. During 1945, Mrs. Ford recognized her husband's mental impairment and protected him from any business talks. . . . In May 1945, Mr. Ford did know and recognize his immediate family, but probably not many others beyond the family. . . . Mr. Ford was doing no reasoning." Henry Ford suffered a series of strokes over the next couple of years and finally, on April 7, 1947, died from a massive cerebral hemorrhage.

Henry Ford brought America into the modern age in the early part of the twentieth century in a way that was breathtaking. Committed to mass production, high wages, consumer values, and a belief in the common man, Ford imagined and then created modern America. In the seminal sociological study *Middletown* (1929), authors Robert and Helen Lynd reported that, for the average American, the automobile had become crucial for "leisure-time as well as getting-a-living activities. . . . Ownership of an automobile has now reached the point of being an accepted essential of normal living." By the 1930s, there were streets and highways crisscrossing America "blooming with garages, filling stations, hot-dog stands, chicken-dinner restaurants, tearooms, tourists' rests, camping sites, and affluence," wrote historian Frederick Lewis Allen. But along with the great innovations came narrow-mindedness, anti-Semitism, anti-intellectualism, and infidelity. Like a double-sided coin depicting Modern America, Henry Ford embodied America's greatest strengths and weaknesses.

EDSEL BRYANT FORD
(1893–1943)

As the only child and heir of Henry and Clara Ford, Edsel wore a heavy mantle. He was a quiet, obedient child more given to music, drawing, and watercolors than mechanical tinkering like his father. He did, however, have an avid interest in cars. In 1903, when Edsel was ten, Henry Ford brought home a bright red Ford Model A runabout—this was the first Model A, not the one issued after the Model T three decades later. Edsel drove the car around the neighborhood and took his mother to do her shopping. At that time, there was no minimum age requirement, nor was a license required for driving. A couple of years later, his father brought him a new Model N. Edsel became very interested in car design.

Edsel Ford skipped college and went right into the family business, learning the ropes and working his way up the ladder. He was well liked by his associates. In 1919, at age twenty-six, Edsel became president of the Ford Motor Company, a post he held until his death in 1943. He married Eleanor Lawthian Clay in 1916, and, unlike his parents, who did not socialize often or easily, the Edsel Fords were very involved in the social orbit of Detroit's elite. They built an estate in the tony town of Grosse Point Shores, outside of Detroit, and also owned homes in Seal Harbor, Maine, and Hobe Sand, Florida, along with a two thousand-acre farm in Michigan. Edsel and Eleanor were art collectors and major benefactors of the arts, particularly in Detroit. Edsel also financed his best friend Admiral Richard Byrd's polar explorations. The first plane Byrd used to fly over the North Pole was named *Josephine Ford*, after Edsel's daughter. (There was controversy over whether or not Byrd actually reached the North Pole. Today, most believe he didn't.) The Fords had four children—Henry II, Benson, Josephine, and William.

When Edsel became president of Ford Motor Company, it was in the throes of building the massive River Rouge industrial complex. Edsel oversaw the construction and made decisions about production and engineering. He was quiet, thoughtful, and articulate in and about his work, unlike his father, who was more prone to making his presence known. According to Henry Ford's biographer, things were not as they seemed. He wrote, "As observers inside the organization gradually discovered, Edsel served as president in name only. His father, though officially in the background, continued to steer the course of the company and make all major decisions. Edsel, ever the obedient and loyal son, swallowed any resentment and acquiesced." Through Edsel's tenure, Henry would undermine and countermand much of his son's authority. Henry Ford wanted to "toughen up" his son, whom he believed was too soft to survive in the cutthroat business of automobile manufacturing. Edsel Ford always displayed the greatest respect for his father in spite of this treatment.

The two Fords had philosophical differences over how the company should be managed. Henry Ford believed that all decisions came down from the top. Edsel Ford believed that with a company as large and complex as the Ford Motor Company, there should be teamwork in managerial decision making. This conflict reached a boiling point in the mid-1920s over the fate of the Model T. Henry Ford loved this affordable car that he had developed for the common man—the car that made the Ford Motor Company what it was. Edsel, however, saw that modern consumers wanted something different, and the Model T had become like an albatross around the neck of the company. The Ford Motor Company's sales were rapidly declining as customers migrated toward other models. After holding out for a couple of years, Henry Ford succumbed to the pressure.

Finally, on May 26, 1927, the new car was announced on the very day the fifteen millionth Model T rolled off the assembly line. Within six months, the first Model As would be rolling off the newly retooled

The Model A was built to replace this car, the Model T. *Source:* Library of Congress.

assembly line. It cost the same as the Model T, but this car, with its sleek design, was so much more. The Model A, which came in a variety of colors, could reach a cruising speed of sixty-five miles per hour and included safety features like hydraulic brakes, safety glass, windshield wipers, and antitheft locks.

In the 1930s, Edsel's artistic sensibilities found an outlet in his partnership with E. T. Gregorie, Ford's automobile designer for the Lincoln luxury line of cars. Both Edsel and Gregorie liked sleek, clean lines, and the two men began working together. Edsel established a design department in the company and installed Gregorie as its head. They worked together on the Lincoln Zephyr line, the Mercury line, and the Lincoln Continental, which together presented consumers with various styles and prices.

By the 1930s, Henry Ford and his son clashed over almost everything. The father disapproved of what he considered his son's lavish lifestyle, his love of art, and his support of the arts. Edsel, who had donated numerous art masterpieces and hundreds of thousands of dollars to the Detroit Institute of Arts, also served as a commissioner of the museum from 1930 until his death. Diego Rivera, the Mexican muralist, came to paint murals on the walls of the art institute's garden court, and the work caused quite a stir when it was finished. Edsel, who had paid for much of the work, defended Rivera's murals, which depicted the dynamic interaction of man with machine in the capital of automobile manufacturing. Rivera spent time in the Rouge River plant in preparation for the mural and his portrayal of man and technology. The controversy was over the Marxist Rivera's depiction of a modern-day "holy family," which offended members of Detroit's religious community, who demanded that the mural be painted over. That didn't happen.

During the Great Depression, Henry and Edsel quarreled over almost everything. Edsel, who believed unionization was inevitable, thought the company should embrace it. Henry fought unionization tooth and nail. Edsel had become friendly with Franklin D. Roosevelt in the 1920s and had even presented him the gift of a new Model A, whereas Henry hated Roosevelt. As Henry Ford became closer with Harry Bennett, the companies security chief, Edsel was pushed even further away.

According to one Ford biographer, by the 1940s, "Henry's mental disintegration was producing outbursts that made the situation unbearable. His criticisms of Edsel became obsessions, and increasingly bizarre directives reflected clouded judgments." At this same time, Edsel began to experience terrible, recurrent stomach pain and vomiting that was resistant to treatment. Henry blamed Edsel's lifestyle—parties, alcohol consumption, and smoking. In January 1942, Edsel had surgery for ulcers, and part of his stomach was removed. Then he developed undulant fever from bacteria found in unpasteurized dairy products. He underwent another stomach surgery in November of that year. The following April, Henry again insisted that Edsel come to terms with Bennett's authority over labor issues, and that he, Henry, would support Bennett against every obstacle. Edsel, although gravely ill, was still working and was at the breaking point. Two weeks later, Edsel collapsed and was taken to his home, where his wife revealed to Henry and Clara that Edsel had been diagnosed with incurable stomach cancer. Henry refused to believe that Edsel was going to die, but for once, Edsel defied his father by dying on May 26, 1943, at the age of forty-nine.

Henry Ford II
(1917–1987)

Henry Ford II, the eldest son of Edsel and Eleanor Ford, was president of the Ford Motor Company from 1945 to 1960, CEO from 1945 to 1979, and chairman of the board of directors from 1960 to 1980. Ford Motor Company became a publicly traded corporation in 1956. He also served as the chairman of the Ford Foundation from 1950 to 1956, an entity created by his grandfather and father, funded entirely by Ford Motor Company stock.

When his father, Edsel, died in 1943, twenty-six-year-old Henry Ford II, a naval officer serving in World War II, was sent home to help run the company. It was deemed to be in the national interest for him to do so (the Ford Company was churning out B-24 bombers to aid the war effort). What Henry II found when he got back to Dearborn was a company—once the pinnacle of automotive manufacturing—in shambles and hemorrhaging money, losing about $9 million every month. First,

Henry II had to wrest control from his grandfather, who, though acting erratically, refused to give up the company he had built and run for over half a century. Fortunately, Henry Ford's wife, Clara, and Henry II's mother, Eleanor, teamed up to sideline the old man, who was running the company into the ground. Company profits between 1931 and 1941 totaled out at zero, and Ford was a distant third in the auto industry, with General Motors as the frontrunner and Chrysler in second place.

The first thing Henry II had to deal with was Harry Bennett, his grandfather's security chief, who had in effect been running the company. Henry II made swift work of dethroning Bennett, who had overseen a reign of terror in the company for a decade by fighting the labor unions and spying on workers. Henry II was officially named president of Ford Motor Company by the board in 1945; however, until Henry Ford's death in 1947, Henry II never felt he had complete power over the company.

Henry II had to take a huge company that, up to that point, had kept scant financial records, had never had an audit, and lacked competent executives in its upper echelons and completely turn it around. Wisely, he hired Ernest Breech, a former General Motors vice president who had become president of Bendix Aviation. Breech arrived in 1946 and reported that he found things "in a pretty sorry state of affairs: $600-and-some-odd million was the total net worth of the company' and the chief engineer 'knew as much about designing cars as a pig did about Christmas,' most of the machines and plants were obsolete, and 'they had financial statements like a country grocery store . . . for a modern business, it was pitiful."

Breech turned the company around, not by bringing out new vehicles but by taking advantage of the seller's market after World War II. "You could sell almost anything you could make, regardless of whether it was any good or not. People just wanted to buy transportation, and admittedly we didn't make a terribly good product." Breech brought some top General Motors executives to Ford Motor Company, and Henry II hired ten young men who had worked as a group in systems analysis for the air force. Known as the Whiz Kids (including Robert S. McNamara), they created the controls that would once again make Ford competitive. During Breech's tenure, in the mid-1950s, the iconic Thunderbird was born.

In 1956, the Ford Motor Company began to publicly trade shares, which was a first for the family-owned and -controled company.

Then in 1957, Ford came out with the Edsel, a car named after Henry II's father, and it was disastrous for the company. Some say it was the styling, and others pointed to the many defects that plagued the early Edsel automobiles. Later, Ford president Lee Iacocca blamed the timing because the Edsel was coming out just as a recession was hitting the country. The Edsel was killed in 1959 after losing up to $350 million.

Like his grandfather, Henry II brought new people into the company and let them go when he didn't like the direction the company was headed. This happened to Breech, then William S. Knudsen (his successor), then Lee Iacocca, who was responsible for bringing out the Ford Mustang in the 1960s and was dismissed by Ford in 1978. In Iacocca's autobiography, he bitterly attacked Ford and wrote that Ford "doesn't want strong guys around."

In 1979, at the annual shareholder's meeting, Henry Ford II said he would retire as CEO and that he was appointing Philip Caldwell, the company's president, as his successor. This was the first time someone from outside the family would run Ford.

Henry Ford II also held a seat on the board of the Ford Foundation from 1943 to 1977, serving as chairman from 1950 to 1956. This family foundation was started by Edsel Ford as a small Detroit charity to administer funds for scientific, educational, and charitable purposes. It was funded by Ford Motor Company stock. In those early days, it supported the Henry Ford Hospital, the Henry Ford Museum, and Greenfield Village. In 1977, the foundation's assets were $2.1 billion (by 2014 that had increased to $12.51 billion). In 1953 the foundation's headquarters was moved to New York City, and the foundation changed its focus to become an international philanthropic organization dedicated to the advancement of human welfare. When Henry II resigned as a trustee, he cited numerous reasons, including the "anti-capitalist undertones in the foundation's work." It wasn't until 2019 that another Ford—Henry Ford III, grandson of Henry II—was elected to the board that bears his family's name.

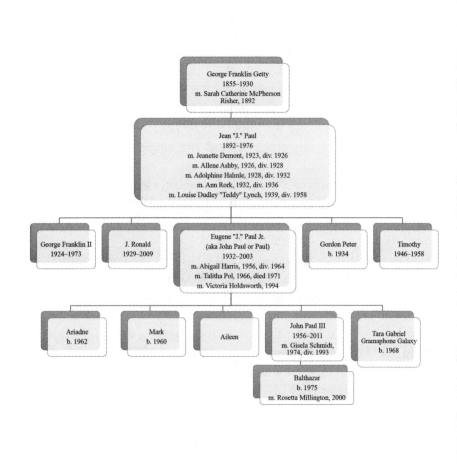

4

Getty

Oil and Art Do Mix

I have 13 other grandchildren, and if I pay one penny now, then I will have 14 kidnapped grandchildren.
—J. PAUL GETTY IN RESPONSE TO BEING ASKED TO PAY A
$17-MILLION-DOLLAR RANSOM FOR HIS GRANDSON

FOR MORE THAN A CENTURY, THE GETTY FAMILY NAME HAS BEEN SYN-onymous with wealth and dysfunction. It's a paradoxical dynasty—a lesson in how wealth can fuel personal pettiness yet drive significant cultural contributions. The family whose name sits on one of the finest museums in the world has conducted a kind of internecine warfare for a century, thanks to the man who played the pivotal role in the Getty saga—J. Paul Getty.

J. PAUL GETTY
(1892–1976)
Called the "wealthiest private citizen in the world" by *Fortune* magazine in 1957, J. Paul Getty (1892–1976) might be best known for his lack of interest in the kidnapping of his grandson and namesake John Paul Getty III. In this telling incident, the older Getty is confronted with what it means to be part of a family, and he does not do well. Young Getty, only sixteen at the time, was living a bohemian lifestyle in a squalid apartment in Rome with his girlfriend (later wife), making art and modeling for photographers. He had grown up in Rome with his mother and three siblings after his parents' divorce. Paul III had been thrown out of yet another private school. His mother, Gail, didn't know what to do

with him—and Paul III refused to live at home because he could not get along with his stepfather, so the teenager was on his own. The Getty name meant money to the outside world, but to young Paul, it was the bane of his existence. His name implied he had money or at least access to money, but in reality, nothing could be farther from the truth. His grandfather had complete control over the purse strings, leaving the family cash poor.

Paul III toyed with the idea of having himself kidnapped to pry some money out of his grandfather, but according to his girlfriend, he had decided not to proceed. After he was nabbed from a public square one warm evening in the summer of 1973, the kidnappers took him to the mountains in Calabria, located in the toe of the boot of Italy, hours from Rome. First, Paul III was kept in an abandoned farmhouse but was eventually moved to a cave in the mountains, where he was chained by the ankle to a stake driven into the floor. The kidnappers demanded $17 million for his release. The request came to his grandfather J. Paul Getty, who made that much money in two hours from his oil wells in the Middle East. But he refused the demand, saying famously, "I have 13 other grandchildren, and if I pay one penny now, then I will have 14 kidnapped grandchildren." The kidnappers, who were part of a mafia group based in Calabria, issued a second ransom note that went unanswered when its delivery was delayed due to a postal strike.

As winter bore down, Getty III endured harsher treatment at the hands of his kidnappers, who began playing Russian roulette with a gun pressed against his head. In November of 1973, a Roman newspaper received a small package containing a lock of hair and a human ear. The note read: "This is Paul's first ear. If within ten days the family still believes that this is a joke mounted by him, then the other ear will arrive. In other words, he will arrive in little bits." The ransom note asked for $3.2 million. Time was critical for the kidnappers because young Getty's wound had become infected, and he then contracted pneumonia. His captors loaded him up with penicillin, gotten from a veterinarian, and then fed him brandy to keep him warm and dull the pain. They knew that a dead young Getty would be worth nothing.

Because he believed everything was open to negotiation, J. Paul responded to the latest ransom note stating he would pay $2.9 million for his grandson's release. He was actually willing to pay only $2.2 million, the maximum amount that was tax-deductible. The richest American in the world then offered to lend his son, John Paul Getty Jr., the boy's father, the remaining $700,000 to use for the ransom. That was to be repaid to the trust that held his inheritance, with 4 percent interest. Shortly after the ransom was paid, Paul III was found alive in a gas station. When his mother suggested he call his grandfather to thank him, J. Paul Getty refused to come to the phone. This wasn't the first or last time the old man turned a rude, cold shoulder to a family member that shared his DNA.

J. Paul Getty had five sons, four of whom lived to adulthood. George Franklin Getty II (1924–1973), the oldest, killed himself the same year young Paul Getty III was kidnapped. Ronald Getty (1929–2009) was the son who would suffer for his mother's acrimonious divorce from his father for the rest of his life. Eugene Paul Getty, also known as John Paul Getty Jr. (1932–2003), was the father of the kidnap victim Paul Getty III. And finally, there was Gordon Peter Getty (b. 1933), poet, composer, singer, and manager of the Sarah C. Getty Trust after J. Paul died. Timothy Getty (1946–1958) died at age twelve. J. Paul Getty married and divorced five times, and most of the boys were half-brothers.

The Getty wealth started, not with J. Paul Getty, the famous miserly owner of Getty Oil, but with his father, George Getty (1855–1930) and his mother Sarah (1852–1941), Midwestern, teetotaling, pious Methodists. The elder Gettys met at The Ohio University, where George was studying to be a teacher. Sarah said she would marry him if he would agree to get a law degree, which he did. They moved to Minneapolis, where George entered the insurance business, and within a few years, the Gettys owned a big house in the most fashionable neighborhood in the growing city as well as a carriage with a beautiful pair of horses. Their daughter Gertrude died at age ten of typhoid. Sarah also contracted typhoid at the same time, leaving her very hard of hearing. She would become stonedeaf at age fifty. George, bereft at the loss of his daughter, flirted with Spiritualism in an attempt to contact Gertrude then and turned away from Methodism and became a Christian Scientist for the rest of his life. In

1892, when Sarah was forty, she found herself pregnant again with their son Jean Paul (1892–1976). Called Paul, his full name was shortened to J. Paul Getty. He was a solitary child, the product of parents who didn't drink, smoke, or socialize and, at their core, were terrified he might get ill and die, according to journalist Russell Miller.

When Paul was ten, George's business took him to Oklahoma, which at that time was still Indian Territory. Oil had just been discovered, and George, wanting to try something new, leased the oil rights on a thousand acres of land for $500 and almost immediately struck oil. Within a year, he had six wells on the lot, and by 1906, Minnehoma Oil (a mash-up of "Minneapolis" and "Oklahoma") made George Getty a millionaire. This windfall prompted the little family to get out of the frigid Midwest and move to sunny California, where they built a mansion on South Kingsley Drive in Los Angeles. J. Paul, who showed very little interest in anything outside of collecting stamps, was sent to a nearby military academy, where for four years he reluctantly marched and drilled.

Eventually J. Paul became interested in girls. He would go on to marry and divorce five times and father five sons by his wives and at least one daughter out of wedlock.

J. Paul, a lackluster student in California, wanted to live in Europe and decided he wanted to attend Oxford. George asked an old friend, William Howard Taft, who happened to be president of the United States, to write a letter of introduction for young J. Paul. With that and his father's money, J. Paul was admitted to Magdalen College at Oxford, where it is unclear if he ever received a degree. He did, however, become friends with wealthy young men who invited him to their homes for weekend house parties. J. Paul became smitten with the privileged English upper class. During the summers, he toured the great capitals of Europe, relishing the art and architecture, all the while receiving a $200-per-month allowance from his father. Finally, George had had enough of his young son's gallivanting, particularly as J. Paul frequently asked for more money. He wanted to start teaching J. Paul the family business and grooming him to be his successor. So George made his son a business proposition; if he came home, he would give him a $10,000 stake to seek his fortune on the Oklahoma oil fields. Any profit would go back into the family business,

Minnehoma Oil, and J. Paul would be given a 30 percent commission. Within two years, J. Paul Getty was a millionaire. He was twenty-three years old.

J. Paul Getty's first marriage was to a seventeen-year-old girl. He was over thirty. Shortly after his first son, George, was born, Getty walked away from his little family. They were soon divorced, and J. Paul's parents were horrified and furious. This pattern would be repeated all too often. J. Paul was a whiz at business. He expanded the oil company to California and renamed it George Getty Oil, Inc. J. Paul threw himself into work, and when his father died in 1930, J. Paul naturally assumed he would inherit the business. However, George finally had his chance to register his displeasure with his son's numerous affairs, marriages, and divorces. Right before his father's death, J. Paul had divorced his third wife and abandoned his second son, Ronald. When the will was read, J. Paul was shocked to discover that the bulk of the estate had been left to his mother Sarah and that his three-year-old son George was to inherit $350,000 and J. Paul a measly $250,000. The father had delivered a stunning blow to his son. J. Paul reacted by doing the only thing that would make George eat his words—he would amass an enormous fortune, enough to make him the richest man in America.

With an initial deposit of almost $3.5 million, Sarah established the Sarah C. Getty Trust as a way to protect the grandchildren (at that time, there were four, Paul Jr. and Gordon having been born to wife number four). Payments were made directly to the grandchildren in care of their mothers, but the amounts were unequal. Ronald received only $3,000 per year because J. Paul despised his ex-wife's family and convinced his mother that Ronald would inherit his ex-wife's family money in the future, according to journalist Miller. This trust would be critical to the health of the Getty family's financial future by safeguarding their rapidly expanding fortune. The Sarah C. Getty Trust would help create the greatest fortune in America. By 1938, J. Paul's personal fortune stood at $12 million. And because he promised his mother he would plow all the profits back into the trust, the value of the Sarah C. Getty Trust stood, just four years after its creation, at $18 million, a nearly sixfold increase on the initial investment.

Over the next decades, J. Paul Getty proved he had the golden touch. He moved the Getty Oil Company forward by leasing oil rights in the Neutral Zone between Saudi Arabia and Kuwait and striking it rich. He also acquired oil companies, refineries, and distributors around the world. He ruthlessly and stealthily bought up stock of competing companies and then added them to his oil empire. A *Fortune* magazine article in 1957 proclaimed J. Paul Getty the richest private citizen in the world. For many years, J. Paul lived in hotels, which suited his peripatetic lifestyle. As he got older, he became more fearful of flying, and after being publicly outed as a billionaire, Getty decided he needed something he hadn't had for years: a home base. He was a committed anglophile and, in 1959, bought a seventy-two-room Tudor mansion called Sutton House not far from London at the bargain price of sixty thousand pounds. Getty lived there for the rest of his life.

J. Paul Getty was famously frugal to the point of oddness. He replied to letters by writing on the paper on which the letter was written and then reusing the envelopes. He installed a payphone in Sutton House because he didn't want his guests or the help using his telephone, according to journalist John Pearson. A renowned and avid art collector, Getty never bought anything unless it was a bargain and, consequently, let some masterpieces slip through his fingers because he thought the price was too high. Fortunately for historians, he kept journals throughout his long life that give a peek into the world of the billionaire. In addition to observations, primarily about art and architecture, Getty noted the cost of every purchase he made, be it a newspaper or a painting by Rembrandt.

In one area of his life, Getty was very aware of what he wanted his legacy to be. In 1948 Getty began donating significant objects from his art collection to the Los Angeles County Museum. Five years later, he created the J. Paul Getty Museum Trust and the following year opened a Getty Museum in his ranch house in Malibu, California. But Getty knew this would only be a stopgap. He intended to build something far grander to host his treasures. When Getty toured Herculaneum (which was buried in ash from the same Vesuvian explosion that buried Pompeii in 79 CE), J. Paul became obsessed with the magnificent half-buried Villa dei Papiri. Getty believed his extensive collection of Greek, Roman, and Etruscan art deserved to be exhibited in a setting more like where they would have been originally displayed, so he hired architects to re-create the villa on his California property. The Getty Villa opened to the public in 1974. Because of his fear of flying, Getty never paid a visit (he had not been to his California home since 1951). He did, however, have lengthy phone calls with the curators, who described every object to him and where they were placed on the property, according to journalist Miller.

When Getty died in 1976, the J. Paul Getty Museum Trust was worth about $700 million, and overnight the Getty Villa became the wealthiest museum in the world. The trustees were obligated to annually spend 4.25 percent of the market value of the endowment on its own programs, which amounted to an enormous sum of money. Eventually, the Getty Center, designed by architect Richard Meier, was built on a hilltop in the Santa Monica Mountains. It opened in 1997 and today houses a magnificent collection of primarily European art, including one of the finest

A pool at the Getty Villa built at J. Paul Getty's property in Malibu. *Source:* Library of Congress.

collections of illuminated manuscripts in the world. The Getty Villa and Getty Center receive nearly two million visitors each year.

In 1976 J. Paul Getty, suffering from inoperable prostate cancer, died in Sutton House in his sleep while sitting upright in a chair. He was afraid that if he lay down in bed, he would die. He was alone. His vast fortune couldn't accompany him in death, but he did make sure that his heirs and the people who surrounded him at the end were left off balance after his death as they had been when he was alive. The little people in his world—his masseur, his security advisor, the gardeners, the butler, and his faithful secretary—got a pittance or nothing. The women in his life— his mistresses, his legal advisor—received monthly allowances in the area of a couple hundred dollars. His longtime companion Penelope Kitson received about $850,000 worth of Getty Oil stock, according to journalist Pearson. The great bulk of his estate covered in the will was wrapped

Designed by Richard Meier, the Getty Center sits in the Santa Monica Mountains. *Source:* Library of Congress.

up in the J. Paul Getty Trust and went to the Getty Museum. The Sarah C. Getty Trust, established forty years earlier by J. Paul's mother, was not covered by the will. This trust determined how its money would be apportioned among the descendants. This unequal distribution of wealth to the family became the source of unhappiness and legal proceedings that would reverberate for decades.

THE HEIRS

Getty's four oldest sons met each other at their grandmother Sarah's house on Christmas Day in 1939. It was the only time the half-brothers would meet as children. J. Paul cut himself off from his sons during their childhood and adolescence, and then he tried to groom them to perpetuate what he called the "Getty dynasty," according to journalist John Pearson. His only interest in his sons revolved around how they conducted Getty business. He never acknowledged or attended any events—like weddings—that involved his sons. When Paul Jr. was twelve, he sent his father a letter. It was sent back, unanswered, but with the spelling and grammatical mistakes corrected. Paul Jr. said, "I never got over that. I wanted to be judged as a human being, and I could never get that from him." When the boys were adults, they suffered from jealousy, bitterness, and nonstop litigation against each other—seeds sown when the Sarah C. Getty Trust was established, giving J. Paul's children differing amounts of money.

At the behest of their father, the sons entered the family business, which now included companies all over the world, from oil fields in the Neutral Zone between Saudi Arabia and Kuwait to refineries in Italy to a Getty-owned company that made mobile homes in Arizona. While working for their father, the sons were moved from pillar to post and endured harsh criticism from the man who could not be pleased. At the same time that J. Paul was trying to micromanage his grown-up sons in the mid- to late 1950s, his youngest son, Timothy, born in 1946 by his fifth and last wife, was undergoing surgeries for a brain tumor that caused the young boy to go blind when he was six. In the summer of 1958, while twelve-year-old Timmy was waiting for what would be his last surgery, he called his father repeatedly, asking him to come to New York to see him. The operation took place on the same day Getty had been invited to see the art collection of Baron Thyssen Bornemisza, whose collection far surpassed Getty's. He did not return his son's phone call, according to Miller. Timmy didn't make it through the surgery, and Getty wrote in his journal: "Darling Timmy died two hours ago, best and bravest son, a truly noble human being. Words are useless." He did not attend the funeral.

While J. Paul was living like a duke in his sixteenth-century Tudor home, his sons, who were always strapped for cash, were not faring as well. Gordon and his wife sued Getty for money from the portion of the trust that would eventually come to them. The terms of the Sarah C. Getty Trust allotted the annual disbursement to each son to be paid in cash or in stock. J. Paul always paid the sons' allotment in stock that was then plowed back into the trust. This left the boys cash poor but exceedingly wealthy on paper. The main reason Getty did this was to avoid paying taxes on the cash, according to Miller. Over his lifetime, in spite of being the wealthiest man in the world at one point, Getty never paid more than $500 in taxes at any one time. As long as the money stayed in the trust, it was untaxable. The complicated lawsuit brought by Gordon dragged on for seven years, and although Gordon lost, J. Paul Getty did eventually pay modest lump sums to his sons. The trust would always be the bane of the Getty boys' existence.

J. Paul Getty's oldest son George Franklin Getty II (1924–1973) was named after his grandfather. George started working for his father at age twenty-three, pumping gas at a Tidewater station. A decade later, George was made president of Getty's Tidewater Oil subsidiary and then operating head of Getty Oil in 1967. But because J. Paul micromanaged every aspect of his many businesses, he never really let George be the boss, according to Pearson. In 1973, George died from an overdose of barbiturates and alcohol, after also stabbing himself in the stomach with a barbecue fork, according to Pearson. His three daughters—known as the Georgettes in subsequent media stories—split George's share of the Sarah C. Getty Trust.

J. Ronald Getty (1929–2009) would always seem like a tragic figure among the cast of characters that make up the Getty story. When J. Paul and his mother Sarah Getty established the Sarah C. Getty Trust, Ronald was six years old. At that point, J. Paul had divorced Ronald's mother, who had returned to her parents' home in Germany when Ronald was born. The divorce was finalized in 1932 with Ronald's mother, Adolphine, or "Fini," receiving full custody and a hefty settlement. J. Paul certainly had this in mind when establishing the beneficiaries of the Sarah C. Getty Trust. Ronald was to be eternally punished by his richer-than-God father, who declared that son was to never receive more than $3,000 annually from the trust.

In 1979, three years after J. Paul's death, Ronald filed a lawsuit to change the terms of the trust. However, a California court declared that he had allowed the California statute of limitations—where the trust was filed—to lapse years earlier. It's not as if Ronald had no money. In 1976, as one of the executors of his father's will, he received $7 million in executor fees. He also received a $10 million settlement from the J. Paul Getty Museum, which settled rather than having a lawsuit drag through the courts. But at the end of the day, his half-brothers never really treated Ronald like he was one of them.

In 1985, the trust, then valued at $4 billion, was divided. One billion dollars was set aside to pay capital gains taxes. The remainder was divided into four smaller trusts of $750 million each. Paul Jr. and Gordon each oversaw their own trusts while George's daughters shared a third. The fourth trust was divided three ways, with Ronald still receiving his $3,000 per year and the rest of the income to be distributed among Ronald's four children. In 1999, Ronald and his wife filed for chapter 7 bankruptcy in a federal court in Puerto Rico, listing $43.2 million in debts.

Eugene Paul Getty, known as John Paul Getty Jr. (1932–2003), was J. Paul's third son and first of his two sons with Ann Rork. After the inevitable divorce, Ann and her sons, Paul and Gordon, moved to San Francisco. After serving in the Korean War, Paul met Abigail "Gail" Harris, the daughter of a San Francisco federal judge, and they were married in 1950. They would eventually have four children before divorcing in 1964. Like his brother, Paul's first job for a Getty company was pumping gas at a Tidewater gas station. J. Paul invited Paul and his family to Paris a year later, where he offered Paul Jr. a job as president of Getty Oil Italiana in Rome. As would be the pattern with all of the sons, J. Paul interfered, micromanaged, and undercut Paul Jr.'s effectiveness in a job he had not been trained to do. Soon after his divorce, Paul Jr. would resign from Getty Oil Italiana.

Two years after his divorce, Paul Jr. married Dutch model Talitha Pol in 1966. Their son Tara Gabriel Galaxy Gramophone Getty was born in 1968. Paul Jr. bought 16 Cheyne Walk in Chelsea, London, where the artist Dante Gabriel Rossetti had lived a hundred years earlier. This house was for Talitha and Tara to live in while Paul Jr. stayed in Rome. Talitha later asked for a divorce in 1971 and went to Rome to meet him. While there, she died of cardiac arrest, according to her death certificate. Paul Jr. fell into a deep depression.

In 1973 Paul Jr. endured the stress of the kidnapping of his eldest son, sixteen-year-old John Paul Getty III. The negotiated settlement included the $700,000 loan from his father to be paid back to the trust with 4 percent interest.

Paul Jr. finally checked himself into the London Clinic in 1984 in an attempt to end his drug addiction. While there, he purchased a run-down country estate west of London called Wormsley Park. Paul Jr. had the Georgian mansion and the three thousand acres of parkland restored. Then he put an addition on his house for his extensive book collection (he had been collecting since he was a child) and added an indoor heated pool and a professional cricket pitch—a game he became enamored with in the 1970s. While at the London Clinic, Paul Jr. began making significant donations of money to the National Gallery.

Because of his donations to the National Gallery, Paul Jr. was appointed Knight of the Order of the British Empire (KBE) in 1987. However, he was not allowed to use the title "Sir" because he was not British. He was granted British citizenship a decade later and became known as Sir Paul Getty for the rest of his life. He was a first-rate book collector and was a notable member of the exclusive Roxburghe Club. In his collection, Sir Paul had a first edition of Chaucer and several Shakespeare folios. He made donations to numerous institutions, including the National Gallery, the British Museum, the British Film Institute, and the Imperial War Museum. At the time of his death in 2003, at age seventy, Paul Jr. was worth over 1.6 billion pounds.

Gordon Peter Getty (b.1934), J. Paul's fourth son and second son by Ann Rork, dutifully worked in the family business, first as manager of the Getty interests in the Neutral Zone, then as a manager of the mobile home division. Both roles were short-lived. Soon Gordon found himself back in his hometown of San Francisco, finishing a degree in music. Gordon was seen as the dreamer of the family—a poet, composer, and singer. But Gordon was not one to take lightly.

Head of the Sarah C. Getty Trust when J. Paul died, Gordon eventually did the unthinkable. He sold Getty Oil to Texaco. With that one act, Gordon Getty increased the trust from $1.8 billion to $4 billion. He then broke the trust into four family trusts, holding out $1 billion to cover the taxes.

In 1999, it was revealed that Gordon had three other daughters by Cynthia Beck, who lived in Los Angeles. The girls wanted their last name to be Getty and had petitioned the court for the name change, which is how the news broke around the world. Gordon released a statement saying they were his daughters and that he loved them very much. His wife, Ann, stuck by Gordon even when it was revealed he had been having the affair for fourteen years. Each of the daughters was given a portion of the trust. He and Ann created a philanthropic organization and, since 2008, have given more than $100 million to the performing arts and to music and museum projects. In 2018 he was worth $2.1 billion.

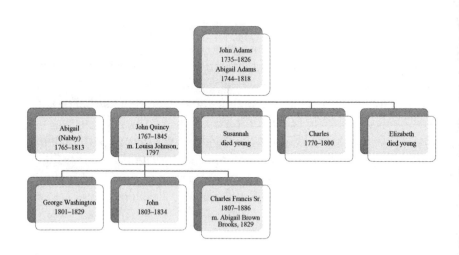

5

Adams

Founding Father and More

His last words were "Jefferson survives."
—John Adams, age ninety, on his deathbed

The Adams family was remarkable for the number of influential politicians, statesmen, and writers it produced in the eighteenth and nineteenth centuries. From the patriarch John Adams, second president of the United States, to his son John Quincy Adams, the sixth president of the United States, to his son Charles Francis Adams, great statesman and ambassador to the Court of Saint James during the Civil War, the Adams family held an outsized influence during some critical times in the early days of this country. From the Revolutionary War to the War of 1812 to the Civil War, an Adams was there, helping to guide the young democracy.

John Adams
(1735–1826)
John Adams was an American statesman, attorney, diplomat, writer, and founding father, who served as the second president of the United States, from 1797 to 1801. Before his presidency, he was a leader of the American Revolution, and he served as the first vice president of the United States under George Washington. Adams kept a daily journal for most of his life and corresponded with many prominent figures in early American history, including his wife and closest adviser, Abigail. His letters and other papers serve as invaluable source material for historical information about the era.

Son of a Congregational minister, John Adams grew up in a comfortable household in Braintree, Massachusetts. As the eldest boy, he was expected to excel at school, which he did, graduating from Harvard, where he had prepared to become a lawyer. While at Harvard, he began writing about events and daily life in a journal, something he did for the rest of his life. Adams was much impressed by lawyer James Otis Jr.'s 1761 legal argument that challenged the legality of British Writs of Assistance, which allowed the British to search a colonist's home without notice or reason. Otis's argument inspired Adams to become a patriot and political activist.

In the late 1750s, Adams fell in love with Hannah Quincy, but he never got up the nerve to propose to her. In 1759, he met fifteen-year-old Abigail Smith, his third cousin, and his first impression of Abigail and her sisters was not a good one. He wrote that they were not "fond, nor frank, nor candid." Later, he grew close to Abigail, and they were married in 1764, despite the opposition of Abigail's mother. John Adams and Abigail shared a love of books and were fortunate that they were able to be honest with each other. In 1761, after John's father died, he inherited a nine-and-a-half-acre farm and a house. This would become John and Abigail's home until 1783.

John and Abigail had six children: Abigail "Nabby" in 1765, future president John Quincy Adams in 1767, Susanna in 1768, Charles in 1770, Thomas in 1772, and Elizabeth in 1777. Nabby, John Quincy, Charles, and Thomas lived into adulthood. All three of his sons became lawyers. Charles and Thomas became alcoholics and died before old age, whereas John Quincy excelled in the law and launched a career in politics. Nabby died of breast cancer. Adams's writings are devoid of his feelings about the sons' deaths; however, he was distraught upon the death of his daughter, Nabby.

As a lawyer and political activist, John Adams was devoted to the right to counsel and presumption of innocence. In 1765, England imposed the Stamp Act on the colonists, forcing them to pay a tax for all stamped documents as a way to finance Britain's war against France. Enforcement of the law was given to British courts rather than colonial courts. Adams railed against the Stamp Act. Using his considerable powers of persuasion, Adams explained that the act should be opposed because it denied two fundamental rights guaranteed to all Englishmen, and, he believed, that all free men deserved. These were the rights to be taxed only by consent and to be tried by a jury of one's peers. The act was soon repealed.

In a turn that would dismay most of his activist friends, Adams successfully defended British soldiers against murder charges arising from their part in the Boston Massacre. He got acquittals for six out of the eight soldiers involved after he reminded the jurors that everyone deserved a fair trial and counsel. Adams main argument was that "If an assault was made to endanger their lives, the law is clear, [the soldiers] had the right to kill in self-defense."

Adams was a Massachusetts delegate to the Continental Congress and became a principal leader of the Revolution. He assisted in writing the Declaration of Independence in 1776 and was its foremost advocate in Congress. Thomas Jefferson wrote the first draft of the document and was later credited as the sole author of the Declaration of Independence. (This led to bad feelings between Adams and Jefferson. And in 1805, five years after he lost a bid for reelection to a second term as president to Jefferson, Adams wondered if there was "ever a coup de théâtre that had so great an effect as Jefferson's penmanship of the Declaration of Independence.")

As a diplomat in Europe, Adams helped negotiate the peace treaty with Great Britain after the Revolution, and he secured vital governmental loans. Adams was the primary author of the Massachusetts Constitution in 1779, which influenced the United States' own constitution and is today the oldest written constitution still in effect in the world.

John and Abigail Adams were inveterate letter writers. John Adams was often away from home—whether to Philadelphia, New York, or Europe, the couple wrote long letters to each other, often about the political business of the day. Abigail, who possessed a keen mind, was her husband's sounding board and his closest advisor throughout their very long marriage.

Adams was elected to two terms as vice president under President George Washington and then, in 1796, was elected as the United States' second president. He was the first and only president elected as a member of the Federalist Party. Adams encountered fierce criticism from what were known as Jeffersonian Republicans and from some in his own Federalist Party, led by his rival Alexander Hamilton. Adams signed the controversial Alien and Sedition Acts and built up the army and navy in the undeclared "Quasi-War" with France. The Quasi-War (French: Quasi-guerre), which broke out at the beginning of Adams's presidency,

was an undeclared war between
the United States and France that
was fought almost entirely at sea
between 1798 and 1800. The newly
established U.S. Navy proved to be
too much for French West Indian
privateers. That, in combination
with the overthrow of the ruling
French government, led the French
foreign minister to reopen negotiations with the United States.
Adams rejected the anti-French
hawks in his own party and offered
peace to France. In 1800, he sent
William Vans Murray to France to
negotiate the terms, and the hos-
tilities officially ended with the

Abigail Smith Adams. *Source*: Library
of Congress.

signing of the Convention of 1800. By the war's end, however, France had
seized more than two thousand American ships.

The main accomplishment of John Adams's presidency was a peace-
ful resolution of the Quasi-War in the face of public anger and Alexander
Hamilton's opposition. During his term, John Adams became the first
president to live in the White House in the nation's new capital, Washington, D.C. He was only there a scant five months before having to
vacate for his successor, Thomas Jefferson.

In his bid for reelection, opposition from fellow Federalists like Alexander Hamilton, and accusations of despotism from Republicans, led to
Adams's defeat by his former friend Thomas Jefferson. Adams retired to
the family farm in Massachusetts, where he would live for the rest of his
life. Eventually, he and Jefferson resumed their friendship and carried on a
correspondence that lasted fourteen years. Between them, they exchanged
158 letters. John Adams died on July 4, 1826—the fiftieth anniversary of
the adoption of the Declaration of Independence. His last words were
"Jefferson survives." What he didn't know was that Jefferson had died a
few hours earlier. At ninety, John Adams was the oldest former president
at his death until Ronald Regan.

John Quincy Adams
(1767–1848)

As the oldest son of John and Abigail Adams, his parents expected great things from John Quincy Adams. And he would not disappoint. Like his father, he was a lawyer, diplomat, statesman, and American president. He also, like his father, kept a journal for most of his long life.

John Quincy Adams would spend his childhood and youth in the company of either his mother or his father, but almost never both. His mother had sole charge of him from age seven to eleven, when his father was first in Europe. Then his father took John Quincy to Europe from eleven to sixteen, while Abigail stayed home with the rest of the children.

By the time John Quincy was seven, the British began to move into Boston, and the people of Boston began to flee. The Adams family lived in Braintree, Massachusetts, seven miles from the little city, and often found themselves accommodating friends, relatives, and even strangers, who told them about privation wreaked upon them by the British. Abigail, who was often alone with the children, lived in almost constant fear. John Adams wrote of George Washington and Benjamin Franklin and Thomas Paine and the calls for independence. The young boy took in, with a deep sense of awe, the great responsibility of public service.

Then John Adams was asked by the Continental Congress to go to France to raise money and troops to help defeat the British. Young John Quincy begged his father to take him with him, and he relented. They crossed the Atlantic Ocean in the middle of winter, running into violent storms and an English warship. The older Adams wrote, "Fully sensible of the Danger, he was constantly endeavouring to bear up under it with a manly courage and patience, very attentive to me, and his thoughts always running in a serious Strain." By the time the Adamses returned to Braintree a year later, John Quincy was fluent in French.

Six months later, John Adams was ordered back to France to negotiate a peace treaty with Great Britain. So off he went, only this time he brought not only twelve-year-old John Quincy but also his younger son Charles, who was only nine, along with a tutor and a private secretary, Francis Dana. John Quincy would not return to America until he was almost eighteen. During that time, he lived in Paris, Leyden, and London, growing into a brilliant young cosmopolite. Finally, it was time for young Adams to go home to get his formal education at Harvard.

In 1790, Adams became a practicing attorney in Boston. Three years later, President George Washington appointed young Adams U.S. minister to Holland. When his father became president in 1797, he appointed his son U.S. minister to Prussia, which meant moving to Berlin. Somewhere in the middle of all the moving, John Quincy found time to travel to England to marry Louisa Johnson, daughter of the first U.S. consul to Great Britain. Although a shy woman, Louisa understood the world of the aristocracy and soon became a fixture on the social scene in Berlin. John Quincy negotiated a maritime treaty with Prussia, but outside of that, he had little to do. When his father lost his bid for a second term as president, John Quincy was recalled from his post immediately.

John Quincy dreaded the thought of returning to work as a lawyer, but he needn't have worried. Over the next several years, he served first in the Massachusetts legislature and then, a year later, was elected to the U.S. Senate. John Quincy supported President Jefferson's Embargo Act and the Louisiana Purchase. In 1809 he returned to the diplomatic corps when President James Madison appointed him as the first officially recognized U.S. ambassador to Russia. While in Saint Petersburg, Louisa became a popular figure at the Russian court. Adams had a front-row seat when the French emperor Napoleon invaded Russia and was soundly defeated by the Russian military. Five years later, Adams was the chief negotiator for the United States during the Treaty of Ghent, which settled the War of 1812. The following year, Adams was appointed as minister to England.

President James Monroe appointed Adams secretary of state from 1817 to 1825. As secretary of state, he acquired Florida for the United States and settled the dispute with Britain over the border between Canada and Oregon Country with the Treaty of 1818. What John Quincy would be most remembered for was his crafting of the Monroe Doctrine in 1823. This doctrine, which stated that the United States would resist any European country's efforts to thwart independence movements in Latin America—including in Argentina and Mexico—would justify U.S. intervention in Latin America later in history.

Five candidates emerged during the presidential election of 1824, each representing different sections of the country. In the Electoral College vote, no candidate had a clear majority, and the election was sent to the House of Representatives. Henry Clay, a Westerner, threw his support toward Adams, who won on the first ballot. Adams did not have the sensibilities of a good politician—he was aloof and stubborn like his father. He did, however, have a vision for the country that included building highways and canals in a massive infrastructure project. He also wanted to survey the entire U.S. coast, build observatories, and establish a uniform system of weights and measures. However, he could get almost nothing through both houses of Congress, which during the midterm election was filled with men favoring Andrew Jackson. Jacksonians thought Adams's proposals smacked of elitism and neglected the common people. The election of 1828 was a bitter fight between Adams and Jackson. Adams lost the election and left Washington without attending Jackson's inauguration, a move reminiscent of his father's reaction to Jefferson's election almost thirty years earlier. A year later, his oldest son George Washington Adams committed suicide, which affected him deeply. George had suffered bouts of depression and "complains of dejections, low spirits and inability to occupy himself," reported his younger brother Charles. George suffered a mental break, and while on his way to Washington from Boston, he grew paranoid and began to hear voices. George argued with passengers on the steamboat traveling through the Long Island Sound and leaped to his watery grave. "My thoughts are so wandering that I distrust the operation of my own reason," Adams wrote in his journal.

John Quincy and Louisa had three sons and a daughter. Their daughter, Louisa, was born in 1811 while they were in Russia but died a long and lingering death about a year later. George (1801–1829) committed suicide, and their second son, John (1803–1834), died from an unknown illness after running up thousands of dollars of debt. John Quincy and Louisa became the legal guardians of their two granddaughters. Adams's youngest son, Charles Francis the only living child after 1834, became the Adamses' political legacy.

The following year, John Quincy was elected to the U.S. House of Representatives, becoming the only person to serve in the House after being president. John Quincy Adams was now focused on fighting slavery and, to that end, defeated a gag rule instituted by Southerners to stifle debate over slavery. In 1841, he argued in front of the Supreme Court on

John Quincy Adams, sixth president of the United States. *Source:* Library of Congress.

behalf of escaped African slaves in the famous *Amistad* case and won the freedom of the captives, who were subsequently returned to the coast of Sierra Leone.

In 1848, Congressman Adams collapsed to the floor of the House of Representatives while arguing that the U.S. government was obligated to honor U.S. Army officers who had served in the Mexican-American War (a war he opposed because he saw it as a war to extend slavery). He had suffered a massive cerebral hemorrhage and died in the Capitol Building two days later.

CHARLES FRANCIS ADAMS SR.
(1807–1886)

Charles Francis Adams carried the heavy mantle of responsibility through the next generation as a historian, editor, writer, politician, and diplomat. In 1810, as a toddler, Charles accompanied his parents to Saint Petersburg, where John Quincy was posted as a diplomat to Russia. George and

John, the older brothers, stayed in Massachusetts with their grandparents. While in Saint Petersburg, Charles's little sister, baby Louisa, was born and died a year later, plunging his parents, particularly his mother, into grief. John Quincy was called to negotiate the Treaty of Ghent after the War of 1812, after which he sent for Louisa and now seven-year-old Charles to meet him in Paris. Louisa and her son and a retinue of servants traveled through the devastation of a post-Napoleonic Europe on a forty-day, two-thousand-mile odyssey.

These early experiences surely had an impact on the precocious Charles Francis, who was reading in French before his fourth birthday. The family, including the two older boys, reunited in London, where John Quincy was posted to serve as minister to Britain. The Adamses stayed for a couple of happy years, with the boys attending school in Ealing, until Adams was called back to the States in 1817 with the election of President Monroe.

Charles Francis attended Boston Latin School and then Harvard College, where he graduated in 1825. Unlike his two older brothers, who greatly disappointed their father by being lackluster students at Harvard—John was kicked out as a senior—Charles found his scholarly footing. But this was only after a disastrous first year when he wrote to his mother of his "depraved habits" and told her he was thinking of leaving school.

After graduation, Charles went to live in the White House with his parents in 1824. There he joined his parents, his brother John, and the three orphaned children of Louisa's sister Nancy. Cousin Mary Catherine Hellen became the object of affection of all the Adams boys. In 1827, according to historian James Traub, she shocked the Adamses by announcing that she and John were going to get married. "Louisa considered neither one suitable for marriage, while her husband, who had only the most minimal expectations of his middle son, appears to have the left the problem to her." Neither George nor Charles attended what was to be the first marriage held in the White House in 1828.

In 1827 Charles moved to Boston to study law with Daniel Webster and then practiced as an attorney in that city. Charles and Abigail Brown Brooks, daughter of a wealthy insurance broker in Medford, Massachusetts, met in Washington the previous year when she was visiting her sister, who was married to a congressman. He proposed in 1827, and his father agreed to the marriage but said the couple had to postpone the wedding for a few years because Charles was only nineteen at the time.

During this time, Charles began writing reviews of books about American and British history for the *North American Review*. He conducted a lengthy correspondence with his father throughout 1827–1828, where he asked the older man to help him develop a "suitably elegant and grave" writing style. John Quincy was thrilled to be able to recommend a reading list to his son, and the two began to discuss, by letter, the great works of literature and the intellectual questions they raised.

In September of 1829, Charles and Abigail Brown Brooks married. Together they were the parents of seven children: Louisa Catherine Adams (1831–1870), John Quincy Adams II (1833–1894), Charles Francis Adams Jr. (1835–1915), Henry Brooks Adams (1838–1918), Arthur George Adams (1841–1846), Mary Gardiner Adams (1845–1928), and Peter Chardon Broods Adams (1848–1927).

Charles Francis served in the Massachusetts House of Representatives from 1840 to 1843, then in the Massachusetts Senate from 1843 to 1845. He bought and became editor of the *Boston Whig* newspaper in 1846, and two years later he ran for vice president as a nominee of the Free Soil Party, on the ticket with Martin Van Buren for president. They lost. He did serve in the U.S. House of Representatives from 1858 to 1860. He later resigned to become U.S. minister to the Court of St. James (ambassador to Britain), following in the footsteps of his father and grandfather. Adams managed to keep Britain neutral during the Civil War, which was no easy task as blockades of Confederate ships were greatly diminishing the cotton supplies to Europe.

Adams returned to Boston in 1869, where he became an overseer (trustee) of Harvard University. Charles also built the first presidential library in the United States. The Stone Library, located at the Adams property Peacefield, contained the fourteen thousand–book library of his father, John Quincy Adams.

Adams's real contribution was in the world of letters. He edited and published several editions of letters of his grandmother and his grandfather. He then took up a project begun by his father. Between 1850 and

Charles Francis Adams, man of letters.
Source: Library of Congress.

1856, he presented ten volumes of *The Works of John Adams, Esq., Second President of the United States*, including John Adams's *Diary and Autobiography* and his political writings, letters, and speeches. This was followed by the *Familiar Letters of John Adams and his wife Abigail Adams, During the Revolution* (1875), released in time for the Centennial Celebration of the American Revolution.

Charles Francis Adams Sr. died in 1886. According to the obituary in the *New York Times*, "he had not been well for some time and had suffered more or less for the past five years from some brain trouble, the result of overwork." It's worth quoting from the last paragraph of the obituary: "Independent and self-reliant to the last degree, no fear of partisan criticism and no considerations of propriety would moderate the expression of a view which he had once formed. At the same time, his temper, not unlike that of his paternal grandfather, caused him to couch his opinion in the most offensive terms and to announce it with scornful indifference to the feelings which it might wound in others. Throughout his career, there are to be seen frequent examples of these traits, which render his undoubted success in diplomacy—the art of all others requiring most self-restraint—the more remarkable."

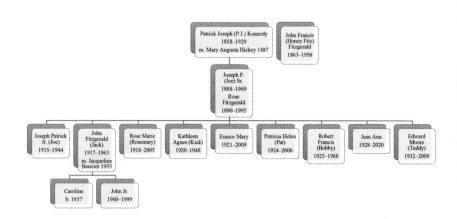

6

Kennedy

America's Brand of Political Royalty

Dear Jack: Don't buy one vote more than necessary. I'll be damned if I'll pay for a landslide.
—Telegram from Joseph P. Kennedy to his son Jack Kennedy when he was running for the Senate

THE KENNEDYS ARE A BIG, MULTIGENERATIONAL IRISH AMERICAN Catholic family with deep roots in Massachusetts. This public-service-oriented family has played a dominant role in the American political system for over a century. They've also found themselves at the center of a series of unfortunate events, including scandals and murders, that is sometimes referred to as the "Kennedy family curse."

PATRICK JOSEPH "P. J." KENNEDY (1858–1929)

Patrick Joseph "P. J." Kennedy and John Francis "Honey Fitz" Fitzgerald were the patriarchs of the multigenerational political dynasty of the Kennedys. Both Kennedy and Fitzgerald were first-generation Americans, as their parents emigrated from Ireland before they were born. Historian Stephen Hess writes, "In the next generation the Fitzgeralds and the Kennedys would be alternately political enemies and allies in the constantly shifting mosaic of Boston politics."

P. J. Kennedy's father died of cholera before he was a year old, so Kennedy grew up as "the man of the house," leaving school at fourteen to help put food on the table. He worked first as a stevedore—the person who loads and unloads cargo from ships—and a longshoreman. Soon he began buying saloons and eventually owned a wholesale liquor company, a coal company, and a local bank.

Kennedy married Mary Augusta Hickey in 1887, and together they would have four children: Joseph, Francis, Mary, and Margaret. When he got married, Kennedy was already serving his third term (out of five one-year terms) as a member of the Massachusetts House of Representatives. He served one term as a state senator. Kennedy became a three-time member of Democratic presidential conventions. An austere man with sandy hair, blue eyes, and a luxuriously curled mustache, Kennedy rarely drank or raised his voice, yet he maintained order. In East Boston, where the Kennedys lived, P. J. was the boss and member of the four-man "Board of Strategy," a powerful, unofficial board of the Democratic Party that picked candidates for mayor and, in essence, ran Boston. In the late nineteenth century, there were more Irish Catholics in Boston—about 60 percent of the population—than there were in Dublin, which gave the Board of Strategy its political clout.

Honey Fitz Fitzgerald, a political rival also on the Board of Strategy, was elected mayor of Boston twice, serving from 1906 to 1908 and from 1910 to 1914—both times without Kennedy's support, who found him insufferable.

The two future in-laws were polar opposites. Kennedy was tall and dignified, and Fitzgerald was short and cocky. Kennedy chose his words carefully, whereas Fitzgerald would talk about anything at any time. According to Hess, in his first two years of office, "Mayor Fitzgerald attended 1200 dinners, 1500 dances, 200 picnics, and 1000 meetings. He made 3000 speeches and danced with 5000 girls." He stuffed city jobs with friends, whether they were qualified or not, and turned a blind eye to funny business dealings between the city and less-than-scrupulous contractors. After being voted out of office after his first term, he worked hard to get elected again, and his second term marked some achievements, including much-needed improvements to Boston's port. Fitzgerald's daughter Rose became his hostess for official events because his wife shunned the public eye.

In 1914, the pretty and deeply religious Rose Fitzgerald (1890–1995) would marry P. J.'s son Joseph P. Kennedy, forever connecting the two most important Irish American Catholic political families of turn-of-the-century Boston. That same year, Fitzgerald did not run for reelection to the office of mayor of Boston when his opponent threatened to publish a newspaper account of Fitzgerald's dalliance with a young cigarette girl, Elizabeth "Toodles" Ryan. She was the same age as his daughter Rose.

Until his death in 1929 at the age of seventy-one, P. J. Kennedy was a behind-the-scenes power broker in Boston. Honey Fitz outlived P. J. by twenty-one years and was alive to see P. J.'s grandson John Fitzgerald Kennedy elected to Congress in 1946. Fitzpatrick died at the age of eighty-seven in 1950, and his funeral was one of the largest in Boston's history.

JOSEPH P. KENNEDY SR.
(1888–1969)

Joseph P. "Joe" Kennedy Sr. was born in Boston in 1888, the son of Patrick Joseph "P. J." Kennedy and Mary Hickey. He had a very comfortable childhood, attending Boston Latin School and then Harvard College. In 1914 he married Rose Fitzgerald, oldest daughter of John F. "Honey Fitz" Fitzgerald and his wife Josie Hannon. Joe and Rose Kennedy would become the parents of nine children—Joseph Patrick Jr. "Joe" (1915–1944), John Fitzgerald "Jack" (1917–1963), Rose Marie "Rosemary" (1918–2005), Kathleen Agnes "Kick" (1920–1948), Eunice Mary (1921–2009), Patricia Helen "Pat" (1924–2006), Robert Francis "Bobby" (1925–1968), Jean Ann (1928–2020), and Edward Moore "Teddy" (1932–2009)—with seventeen years between the oldest, Joe Jr., and the youngest, Teddy.

Joe Kennedy Sr. was ambitious, both for himself and his children. By his mid-twenties, he was already wealthy, having made a small fortune in commodities and stock trading. His timing was perfect—he knew when to buy and sell to gain the most profit. He preserved his fortune by getting out of the market right before the crash in 1929. Later, he explained that he knew when to make his move when the shoeshine boy started giving him stock tips that were right on the mark. Kennedy decided that if the shoeshine boy knew, then everyone knew, and that couldn't be a good sign.

In the mid-1920s, Joe Kennedy got into the movie business. He invested in a chain of New England movie theaters, which led him to

Joe Kennedy, kingmaker. *Source:* Library of Congress.

Hollywood and the production side of the business. He moved to California in 1928, where he worked with a series of production companies that led to the merger that created RKO. While in Hollywood, he began a three-year affair with actress Gloria Swanson, for whom he produced several silent films. (Joe Sr. had numerous extramarital affairs besides the one with Gloria Swanson, including one with Marlene Dietrich, according to Kennedy historian Stephen Hess.)

In 1933, Joe Sr. and Rose Kennedy accompanied Mr. and Mrs. James Roosevelt (son and daughter-in-law of President Franklin D. Roosevelt) to Europe. While there, Joe Sr. and Jimmy Roosevelt met with salesmen for English distilleries. Joe Kennedy returned home as the U.S. agent for Haig and Haig, John Dewar, and Gordon's Gin. Although Prohibition was still in effect in the United States, Kennedy was able to get the whisky and gin shipped to his warehouses in the States under "medicinal" licenses issued in Washington. When the 21st Amendment repealing Prohibition passed later that year, Kennedy's firm, Somerset Importers, was ready. He had bought the business for $100,000 and, in 1946, sold it for $8 million in cash.

Joe Kennedy Sr. became one of America's wealthiest individuals. In 1957 *Fortune* magazine estimated his fortune at above $250 million, on par with Irenee and William DuPont, Howard Hughes, and Sid Richardson. And Joe Sr. didn't manufacture anything—his name wasn't on any product. His investments in the stock market, the film industry, the liquor business, and real estate made him extremely wealthy. He worked hard so that his children did not have to go into the business world as he did. He wanted them to enter public service.

During World War I, Joe Sr. was an assistant general manager of a Boston-area Bethlehem Steel shipyard. Franklin D. Roosevelt was the assistant secretary of the navy, and the two ambitious young men got to know one another. By the time Roosevelt ran for the office of president, Kennedy was a major donor to the Democratic Party. Roosevelt realized how important Kennedy's support could be in capturing the Irish Catholic vote, and Kennedy was happy to oblige because he expected Roosevelt to reward him by appointing him secretary of Treasury, according to this source. That didn't happen. Instead, Roosevelt made Kennedy head of the U.S. Securities and Exchange Commission (SEC), which he ran for a couple of years. To some, this seemed like putting the fox in charge of the henhouse, given Kennedy's killing in the market right before the 1929 crash, but Kennedy did a great job at the SEC. Then President Roosevelt appointed Kennedy to be the first chairman of the Maritime Commission.

In 1938, though, Roosevelt handed Kennedy a plum when he appointed him ambassador to the Court of St. James.

Joe and Rose and their nine children went to London, where they took the city by storm. The British were entranced with the new ambassador and his spirited brood that played football on the lawn of the ambassador's house next to Kensington Palace. The Kennedy girls were presented at court. It was said that when Joe Sr. was appointed ambassador, England got eleven ambassadors for the price of one.

England was grappling with whether or not to enter the war that was beginning to spread through Europe. Kennedy supported Prime Minister Neville Chamberlain's policy of appeasement, finding that some diplomatic terms that Adolph Hitler agreed would avoid conflict between England and Germany. Kennedy also did not think that the United States should get involved with the war in Europe, and in an op-ed in the *Boston Sunday Globe* in 1940 he wrote, "Democracy is finished in England. It may be here." As Britain endured the Blitz—the nightly bombing raids by Germany during 1940 and 1941—Kennedy became increasingly more defeatist. After Roosevelt took office for a third term, Kennedy submitted his resignation as ambassador and returned to the States.

Joe Sr. entertained thoughts of throwing his hat into the presidential ring in 1940 when he thought Franklin D. Roosevelt wouldn't be standing for an unprecedented third term (there was not yet a constitutional amendment stating that a president could only serve for two terms). However, Roosevelt did put himself up for reelection and that, coupled with Kennedy's controversial judgment while serving as U.S. ambassador to the Court of St. James, put an end to his personal political ambitions. Then he turned his attention toward his oldest sons, Joe Jr. and Jack.

But the war years would have a devastating impact on the Kennedy family. In 1941, Joe Sr. took twenty-three-year-old daughter Rosemary to have a frontal lobotomy that he hoped would alter her behavior. Rose Kennedy was not consulted. Rosemary had developmental delays and was becoming difficult for Rose and the family to manage as she got older. As a result of the operation, Rosemary was left permanently incapacitated. She was placed in an institution where she lived for the rest of her life.

Her name was not mentioned in the house, and Rosemary's siblings did not know where she was until twenty years later.

Joe Jr. became a navy bomber pilot in World War II. He volunteered to pilot a bomber to Germany packed with explosives that would be guided by remote control once he and the copilot parachuted to safety. The plane exploded over the English Channel, and all aboard were killed. Jack also enlisted in the navy and served in the Pacific as commander of a PT (patrol torpedo) boat that was rammed by a Japanese explorer in 1943. He and eleven of the crew survived, but for the rest of his life, Jack Kennedy suffered from excruciating back pain as a result of his injuries. In 1944, Kick who had remained in England to work in a Red Cross canteen, married William "Billy" Cavendish, the oldest son of the Duke of Devonshire. Rose Kennedy was opposed to the marriage because Cavendish was Protestant. They were married for only a month when Billy Cavendish was killed in action. Kick died a few years later when the small plane she was traveling in crashed. The deaths of Joe Jr. and Kick plunged the family into grief and action. Historian Stephen Hess quotes a friend of the Kennedys who said in 1957, "The boys are trying to live up to the image of Joe as they remember him. . . . The girls feel the same obligation to emulate Kathleen."

During the 1950s, Joe Sr. turned to the political careers of his sons Jack and Bobby, and eventually Ted. He used his influence, connections, and wealth to promote his sons and get them elected to the Senate and the presidency. In 1961, after his son Jack was elected president, Joe Sr. suffered a debilitating stroke that would leave him paralyzed on his right side and unable to speak. He lived eight more years, long enough to see two of his sons assassinated and the third derailed from his presidential ambitions by his involvement in the death of a woman in Chappaquiddick, Massachusetts.

THE BROTHERS

John Fitzgerald Kennedy (1917–1963), Robert Francis Kennedy (1925–1968), and Edward Moore Kennedy (1932–2009)

The third generation of Kennedys included the three brothers who would define a political generation (or two). Underpinned by privilege, wealth, and political influence, these three Kennedy men would dedicate their lives to public service.

Like their father, the three Kennedy brothers attended private schools and then graduated from Harvard University. Then Bobby and Teddy continued at the University of Virginia, where both received law degrees. Jack Kennedy graduated from Harvard in 1940, and his senior thesis was about appeasement and British participation in the Munich Agreement. Retitled *Why England Slept*, it was a bestselling book selling eighty thousand copies in Britain and the United States that first year.

Jack Kennedy's service in World War II, from 1942 to 1945, garnered him numerous medal's including a Purple Heart and the Navy and Marine Corps Medal. The problem for Jack was what to do after the war. He liked journalism and history, and his path would likely have led him to that of college professor or the media; but then his brother Joe Jr. died, and his father's political hopes shifted to Jack.

In 1946 a congressional seat opened up in Boston, one previously held by Jack's grandfather Honey Fitz. The Eleventh Congressional District was overwhelmingly Democratic and contained the former strongholds of both grandfathers, P. J. Kennedy and John Fitzgerald. Jack was elected by a land-

John F. Kennedy, 35th president of the United States. *Source:* Library of Congress.

slide. In 1952, Republican Henry Cabot Lodge Jr. came up for reelection in the Senate, and Joe Sr. encouraged Jack to challenge Lodge. All of the Kennedys campaigned for the young congressman. Bobby became his campaign manager (Teddy was in the army from 1951 to 1953 and was in

Germany at the time). The Kennedy women held tea receptions in every corner of the state. Bobby's wife Ethel made a speech just before the election and then drove to Boston and had a baby. And Joe Sr. bankrolled the enterprise. It became clear that the Kennedys presented a united and formidable political challenge, one that would repeat itself several times in the future. Jack beat Lodge by over seventy thousand votes, even though Republican Dwight Eisenhower won the presidency.

In 1953 Jack Kennedy married Jacqueline "Jackie" Bouvier, in a Newport wedding. Her father was a stockbroker, and her stepfather Hugh Auchincloss Jr. was an heir to the Standard Oil fortune. A graduate of George Washington University and fluent in French and Spanish, Jackie would prove to be a memorable First Lady, who refurbished and restored the White House and brought style and graciousness to her role. The Kennedys would have four children, two of whom died at birth.

Bobby married Ethel Skakel in 1950. Ethel had been his sister Jean's roommate at Manhattanville College of the Sacred Heart. Ethel's father was a self-made millionaire. Bobby and Ethel would have eleven children. Ethel was a crackerjack campaigner for all of the Kennedys and became an important social activist. (In 2014, President Obama awarded her the Presidential Medal of Freedom for her dedication to advancing the cause of social justice, human rights, environmental protection, and reduction of poverty.)

Teddy married twice. He met Joan Bennett at Manhattanville College of the Sacred Heart when he was attending a dedication to his sister Kathleen. His sister Jean introduced Joan to Ted. They married in 1958 and then divorced in 1983. Ted and Joan had four children, one of whom was stillborn. Bennett later told *McCall's* magazine about her chronic alcoholism and how that contributed to the failure of the marriage.

Almost a decade later, Teddy married Vicki Reggie, an attorney. Reggie grew up in Louisiana, and the Reggies and John Kennedy were friends. Ted met Vicki—a single mother of two—at a party for her parents' fortieth wedding anniversary in 1991, and they married in 1992.

When Senator John Kennedy took his seat in 1953, he was not the only Kennedy in the Senate chamber. Bobby was the new associate counsel of the Senate Permanent Investigations Subcommittee under the direction of Joe McCarthy, the senator from Wisconsin. The Kennedys liked McCarthy. But Bobby resigned from the McCarthy Committee because of a personality clash with chief counsel Roy Cohn. He rejoined the committee as minority counsel to the Democrats.

Bobby Kennedy, before his assassination in 1968 while running for president. *Source:* Library of Congress.

During his first couple of years as senator, Jack underwent several spinal operations and was often absent from the Senate. In 1956 he published *Profiles in Courage*, a series of essays on political courage as displayed by American senators. It was an instant success, and the book went on to win the Pulitzer Prize. Ted Sorensen, Kennedy's close adviser and speechwriter, confirmed that he co-wrote the book with Kennedy in his 2008 autobiography *Counselor*.

Jack Kennedy gave the nominating speech for Adlai Stevenson at the 1956 Democratic Convention, which placed the young, charismatic Kennedy on the American stage. He ran for reelection to the Senate in 1958, which he won, and in January 1960 he threw his hat in the ring for the Democratic presidential nomination. All of the Kennedys took to the campaign trail in support of Jack. Once again, Bobby Kennedy became Jack's campaign manager, and his father bankrolled the campaign. At one point, Jack told a New York audience that he had received the following wire from his father: "Dear Jack: Don't buy one vote more than necessary. I'll be damned if I'll pay for a landslide."

Kennedy chose Texas senator Lyndon B. Johnson as his running mate, in part to shore up support in the South. His Republican opponent was Richard M. Nixon. A major issue during the campaign was Kennedy's Catholicism, and the candidate brought the topic up time and again, stressing that he was a Democratic candidate who happened to be a Catholic. The turning point in the election was the televised debate against Nixon. Kennedy appeared calm and relaxed, whereas Nixon was sweating and had a "five o'clock shadow," making him look nervous and uncomfortable. Jack Kennedy won by two-tenths of one percent of the popular vote but by 303 to 268 Electoral College votes. At age forty-three, John Fitzgerald Kennedy, the thirty-fifth president, became the youngest person to be elected to the office.

One thing that Joe Sr. wanted Jack to do was to appoint his brother Bobby as attorney general, which he did. Bobby had no experience practicing law, and Yale law professor Alexander Bickel wrote, "On the record, Robert F. Kennedy is not fit for office." Later, in a quip to a group that Bobby did not think was funny, Jack said, "I can't see that it's wrong to give him a little legal experience before he goes out to practice law."

Bobby, who surrounded himself with the best legal minds, served as the president's trusted adviser and lightning rod.

During Jack Kennedy's short term in office, there were definite high and low points. In November 1961, he authorized a covert CIA operation to overthrow the Cuban government of Fidel Castro in the disastrous Bay of Pigs invasion. Kennedy also authorized Operation Mongoose, a secret program against Cuba aimed at removing the communists from power. In October 1962, U.S. spy planes discovered a Soviet ballistic missile deployment in Cuba, and for thirteen days, the United States was on the brink of nuclear war. Cuba lies only ninety miles off Florida, and ballistic missiles would be able to hit any target along America's East Coast. On October 22, Kennedy put a naval blockade in place to prevent offensive weapons from being delivered to Cuba and also demanded that weapons already in Cuba be dismantled and sent back to the Soviet Union. President Kennedy and Soviet leader Nikita Khrushchev negotiated an agreement, resulting in the dismantling of the weapons and a promise that the United States would not invade Cuba again. The United States also agreed to dismantle ballistic missiles it had deployed in Turkey against the Soviet Union. One other result of the Cuban Missile Crisis was the establishment of the hotline between Washington and Moscow.

President Kennedy established the Peace Corps, naming his brother-in-law Sargent Shriver as its first director. He also promoted the Apollo space program with the promise he made to Congress of "landing a man on the Moon by the end of the decade and returning him safely to Earth." Kennedy also supported the civil rights movement, and Congress passed many measures of his New Frontier domestic policies, including an increase in Social Security payments, an increase in the minimum wage, and the extension of aid to children of unemployed workers.

Jack Kennedy's personal life was riddled with numerous affairs before and after he was married, including during his time as president. Women linked to Kennedy include Marilyn Monroe, Judith Campbell, Marlene Dietrich, Mimi Alford, and Pamela Turnure. These indiscretions were well-known by the press, who shielded the president from scandal.

Meanwhile, Joe Sr. was determined to get his youngest child, Ted, established in politics. Ted wanted the Senate seat vacated by Jack when he was elected president, and with the help of his father's deep pockets, he won the election by a two-to-one vote in 1962. Ted would hold this seat until his death in 2009. Although he tried running for president several times, he never got the nomination because of the baggage he brought to the campaigns.

On November 22, 1963, while in a motorcade on his way to deliver a speech in Dallas, John F. Kennedy, the youngest elected president of the United States, was murdered. The country was plunged into shock, and as it struggled to right itself, Lyndon B. Johnson, Kennedy's vice president, was given the oath of office. After a state funeral patterned on that of Abraham Lincoln, Jackie Kennedy and her two young children moved out of the White House.

In June 1964, a small plane carrying Senator Ted Kennedy and several others to the Massachusetts Democratic convention crashed in an apple orchard. Several people were killed, and Kennedy suffered a broken back. He was immobilized for five painful months before he could return to the Senate.

Bobby Kennedy, who felt lost after his brother Jack's death, had to figure out what to do next. He decided to run for the Senate from the state of New York. The Kennedys had lived in New York when the children were young, but that was decades earlier. However, anxious to get a Democratic senator elected, the New York State Democratic party let him run as their candidate. This gave all of the grieving Kennedys something to do. They cranked up the election machine that had worked so well for earlier Kennedy elections, and family members crisscrossed New York State, giving speeches and meeting the public. At the same time, the Kennedy family was campaigning for Teddy, who won by eight hundred thousand votes. Edward M. Kennedy of Massachusetts, who had been elected to his first full term, and Robert F. Kennedy of New York were sworn in as U.S. senators on January 4, 1965. It was only the second time in the Senate's history that two brothers served at the same time.

In 1968, Bobby Kennedy decided to run for president. He hesitated in announcing his candidacy because he believed that Johnson was going to run for another term. However, on March 31, Johnson announced that he would not seek reelection. Vice President Hubert Humphrey was the administration's candidate, but it was too late for him to run in any primaries. Kennedy's opponent in the primaries was Senator Eugene McCarthy of Minnesota. If Kennedy could defeat McCarthy in the California primary in early June, he would be in a good position to challenge Humphrey at the Democratic National Convention in Chicago.

Bobby Kennedy scored a major victory over McCarthy in California. Kennedy was celebrating with his supporters in the Ambassador Hotel in Los Angeles when he was shot three times at close range. He died two days later.

Teddy Kennedy was the last living son of Joseph and Rose Kennedy, which must have been a heavy mantle for the young man to bear. A year after Bobby's death, Ted Kennedy was driving Mary Jo Kopechne, a former campaign aide, from a party on Chappaquiddick Island in Massachusetts when the car he was driving plunged into a pond after skidding off a bridge. Kennedy swam free from the sinking car and later said that he tried to rescue Kopechne from the submerged car but couldn't. He

Ted Kennedy, longtime senator from Massachusetts. *Source:* Library of Congress.

left the scene and didn't report the accident to the police until the next morning. Kennedy pleaded guilty to leaving the scene of an accident and received a two-month suspended jail sentence. Several months later, an inquest concluded that Kennedy was operating his vehicle negligently, but a grand jury returned no indictments. His driver's license was suspended for sixteen months after the accident.

The Chappaquiddick incident really prevented Ted Kennedy from becoming president. He ran once, in 1980, and lost the nomination to incumbent president Jimmy Carter. Ted was reelected seven times to the U.S. Senate, where he was a champion of social and economic justice. He and his staff wrote over three hundred bills that became law, including the COBRA health insurance provision, the Americans with Disabilities Act, the Civil Rights Act of 1991, and the No Child Left Behind Act. Kennedy was respected by senators on both sides of the aisle for his rhetorical eloquence. Ted Kennedy died of a malignant glioma brain tumor in 2009 and was buried near his brothers in Arlington National Cemetery.

II

Money

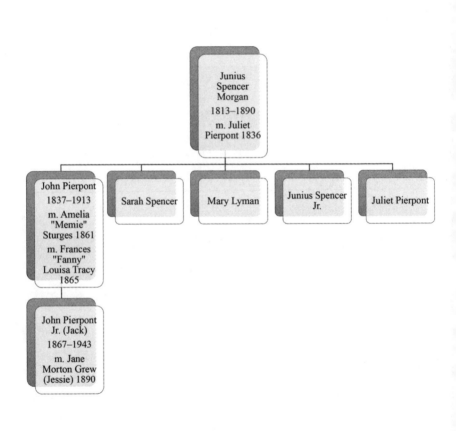

7

Morgan

Managing Money

Let what you now witness make an impression not to be eradicated..
. slow &, sure should be the motto of every young man.
— JUNIUS SPENCER MORGAN IN A LETTER TO HIS SON
J. PIERPONT MORGAN

THE NAME MORGAN IS SYNONYMOUS WITH MODERN AMERICAN BANK-
ing and the world of high finance, but what most people don't remember
(or know) is that the Morgan family has had a hand in shaping America's
fortunes for almost two hundred years.

JUNIUS SPENCER MORGAN
(1813–1890)

The Morgan story is not one of rags to riches—father, son, and grandson did not have to claw their way to the top. The first Morgan came
to America from Wales in 1636, and by the time Junius was born, the
family had amassed some wealth and good manners. In 1817 Junius's
father Joseph moved the family to Hartford, Connecticut, from West
Springfield, Massachusetts, where he founded the Aetna Fire Insurance
Company. A disastrous fire in the Wall Street area of lower Manhattan
destroyed over six hundred buildings in 1836. Morgan paid his customers promptly, putting the firm on solid footing on Wall Street and with
future customers, allowing him to reap a nice windfall when he tripled
Aetna's premiums. That same year, twenty-three-year-old Junius married
Juliet Pierpont, daughter of the fiery Unitarian preacher Reverend John
Pierpont of Boston.

At the time of his son's marriage, Joseph Morgan set Junius up with a partnership in the Hartford dry-goods house of Howe and Mather. Junius cashed in his stake in the company for $600,000 in 1847 when his father died and left him a million dollars. He joined J. M. Beebe, Morgan and Company—Boston's largest import/export/jobbing house—as a partner, where he financed and exported cotton and other goods that traveled by clipper ships to Europe. This is how Junius Spencer Morgan came to the attention of George Peabody.

George Peabody was an American expatriate living and working in London. He founded a firm—George Peabody and Company—that chased down money owed from individual American States to England. Early in the American Republic, the United States, in its push west, built turnpikes and canals and railroads, all of which were backed by State credit. The credit was the result of bonds purchased in London. When Peabody moved to London in 1837, a number of States were refusing to pay the interest on their debts. Peabody became the middleman between the States and the British financiers and was able to renegotiate most of the loans.

Peabody joined the ranks of merchant bankers who dealt in "high finance" that served only governments, large companies, and wealthy individuals. These bankers financed overseas trade, issued stocks and bonds, and dealt in commodities. Peabody, a bachelor, did not have an heir, and as he entered his late fifties, this began to weigh on him. What would become of his business? He began to search for a sociable American with a family who had international business experience.

When Junius Spencer Morgan and his family—a wife and five children—visited London in 1853, he sat down with George Peabody. Peabody liked what he saw. Historian Ron Chernow describes Morgan as "tall with sloping shoulders and the thickening midriff of a strong but sedentary man. . . . He was witty and genial, but a deep reserve and watchfulness lay behind the charm. . . . Big and brooding, he was the sort of prematurely middle-aged young man old financiers found consoling." Peabody had capital of 450,000 pounds in the business and offered Morgan a ten-year partnership, at which point he would retire and leave the business to Morgan. Peabody also indicated he would include some money if Morgan felt he had not accumulated a reasonable amount of capital over the decade. Junius took the job and moved the family to London in 1854.

It's hard for us to imagine the chaotic American banking system in the first half of the nineteenth century. There was no uniform currency: each state had a separate banking system, and within each state, local banks could print their own money. It was impossible to spend local currency when traveling because there was always the possibility that it was counterfeit. It wasn't until "greenbacks," or U.S. dollars, were issued by the federal government during the Civil War that you could be reasonably sure that the dollar you held in your hand was legitimate. This chaos was the American side of the financial world George Peabody and Company dealt with. Additionally, panics or downturns in the market had a profound effect on financial services companies. The panic of 1857 nearly did the company in as wheat prices tumbled and American banks began to falter. Peabody would have gone under if the Bank of England had not extended the company additional credit. This taught Morgan to always take the safe bet. As he wrote to his son Pierpont, "Let what you now witness make an impression not to be eradicated . . . slow & sure should be the motto of every young man."

Junius Morgan assumed control of George Peabody and Company in 1859 as Peabody, who was unwell, decided he wanted to travel. During the American Civil War, Morgan traded in Union bonds, which rose and fell depending upon the outcome of each battle. As the war progressed, Junius's son Pierpont—who worked for Peabody's American agent, the New York bank Duncan, Sherman & Company—began sending telegrams to his father in code and by way of Nova Scotia. This was to avoid telegraph operators reading and then selling the information to others in the cutthroat bond business. Junius began to know the outcome of each battle before other London merchant bankers did, allowing him to buy or sell to make a profit, according to Chernow. At the time, this was not illegal; however, today these telegrams would be considered insider trading.

In 1864, George Peabody retired and gave Morgan the business but wouldn't allow Morgan to use the company name. This was a blow to Morgan, who knew that the merchant banking business was built and run on reputation. Without the Peabody name, he was at a disadvantage. He reluctantly changed the name to J. S. Morgan & Company.

Junius Morgan got his chance to cement his reputation in 1870. During the Franco-Prussian War, France was desperate for financing after being trounced by German troops. The balance of power was delicate in Europe, and other merchant banks, like Rothschild's, didn't want to pump money into what they saw as a lost cause. Morgan floated a ten million pound ($50 million) loan to France. A brief history of the Morgan Bank notes, "Some communications between Paris and London were implemented by the use of a fleet of carrier pigeons. . . . One particularly bulky package of documents was sent from Paris to London by balloon!" When the war ended, even though the French lost, they repaid their loan, and by 1873 Morgan had made a whopping 1.5 million pounds on his gamble.

Morgan was now the wealthiest American banker in London, and he lived like it. He bought a mansion in London and an estate outside of town. He filled both with valuable pieces of art, including paintings by Reynolds, Romney, and Gainsborough. On his estate of rolling hills and carefully tended lawns and gardens, he relished the role of the country gentleman. His wife, Juliet Pierpont Morgan, was not faring as well. She split her time between England and New York and, over the years, became feeble and withdrawn. She spent decades living like an invalid. Junius S. Morgan would have numerous affairs during his marriage, and as his wife withdrew, his affairs became more noticeable. During the 1870s, Alice Mason, twenty-five years his junior and a full year younger than his son Pierpont, became his traveling companion. In 1884, Juliet suffered a seizure and died, leaving Junius free.

As Junius aged, he loved to travel throughout Europe and collect art. Every winter, he spent at least three months in Rome, accompanied by Alice Morgan and various family members. On April 5, 1890, the elderly Morgan, now seventy-six, was in Monte Carlo and riding in a Victoria carriage when the horse was spooked by a passing train. Morgan stood up and fell from the carriage, hitting his head on some rocks. The old man lingered for several days before dying. Junius Morgan left most of his estate to his son Pierpont, which, excluding the art, came to about $15 million (over $400 million today). He left Alice Mason an annual income of $5,000 (worth over $140,000 today), and his daughters received cash and trusts equaling about $3.5 million (almost $100 million today).

JOHN PIERPONT MORGAN
(1837–1913)

The oldest son of Junius Spencer Morgan and Juliet Pierpont, Pierpont, as he preferred to be called, had a nomadic childhood, moving between Hartford, Connecticut, and Europe. He was a sickly child, and when a bout of rheumatic fever at age fifteen left him almost unable to walk, he was sent to the Azores to recover. While there, he was homesick and regularly wrote to his mother, to whom he was very attached. When he returned to the States, he attended the English High School of Boston, where he excelled at mathematics. Because his father recognized the value of learning some European languages, especially when working in the financial world, he sent Pierpont to Switzerland to learn French and then to the University of Gottingen in Germany, where he received a degree in art history. Finally, at age twenty, when Pierpont was ready to go to work, there was no question that he would be working in banking for his father.

In 1858 Pierpont went to work at Duncan, Sherman & Company, the American representatives of George Peabody and Company in New York City. He "volunteered" so he could learn the ropes, but his father paid him $200 a month.

Junius Morgan was an exacting taskmaster, especially when it came to his son Pierpont. One journalist described their relationship: "The Morgans always believed in absolute monarchy. While Junius Morgan lived, he ruled the family and the business—his son and his partners." Until Junius died, in 1890, he dominated his son's life. Although he was genial, he employed an iron discipline.

From 1860 to 1864, Pierpont acted as the American agent in New York for his father's firm, J. S. Morgan & Company, after George Peabody's retirement. In the spring of 1861, Pierpont took part in a business deal that would provoke years of controversy. The Union Army was desperate for firearms. Morgan financed the purchase of five thousand surplus rifles, known as Hall Carbines, at $3.50 each, which were then bored out to turn them into fifty-eight-caliber weapons. The boring of each rifle cost 75 cents. The rifles were then sold to field general John C. Fremont for $22 each. Much was made of buying guns from the government and then selling them back to the government for a hefty profit. Morgan's involvement in the affair slightly tarnished his reputation when the Congressional Committee on Government Contracts issued a report highly critical of arms merchants in 1863. Pierpont was also chastised for paying a substitute $300 to serve in his stead during the Civil War; however, at this time this was a common practice among men who could afford it.

In October of 1861, Pierpont married Amelia "Memie" Sturges. A week before the wedding, Memie was taken ill with fits of "paroxysmal coughing." While on their honeymoon to Europe, Memie was diagnosed with tuberculosis, which was a death sentence in the nineteenth century. In February 1862, Memie Sturges Morgan died in Nice, France. Her body was brought back to Fairfield, Connecticut, where she was buried. The twenty-four-year-old Pierpont never fully got over the loss of his first wife.

Morgan's world brightened three years later in 1865 when he married Frances Louisa Tracy, known as Fanny. They honeymooned in Europe, where Fanny discovered she was pregnant with their first child, Louisa (1866–1946). They would have three more children: John Pierpont Morgan Jr. known as Jack (1867–1943); Juliet Pierpont Morgan (1870–1952); and Anne Tracy Morgan (1873–1952). Like his father, Pierpont eventually became estranged from his wife (divorce seemed to be out of the question) and engaged in many extramarital affairs. Although Pierpont tried to suppress the gossip about his escapades, the Morgan estrangement was no secret.

Between 1864 and 1895 and the formation of J. P. Morgan & Company, Pierpont worked with several men whom he considered his mentors, including Anthony J. Drexel. Morgan partnered with the Drexels of Philadelphia to form the New York firm of Drexel, Morgan & Company.

The House of Morgan on Wall Street. *Source:* Library of Congress.

And after his father's death in 1890, Pierpont gained control of the London-based company J. S. Morgan & Company.

The name Morgan in the late-nineteenth and early-twentieth centuries became synonymous with business mergers, takeovers, and corporate reorganizations. Pierpont became deeply enmeshed in financing and reorganizing a railroad empire that would stretch across the United States. Morgan saw that railroad competition and the accompanying rate wars and parallel building of rail lines was destroying confidence in U.S. and foreign markets. Consequently, he put all of his professional energies into stabilizing railroad finance and maintaining the flow of investment capital from Europe. His concern was the country's long-term economic future. Fixing shipping rates and stifling competition did not please everyone. Farmers and shippers of goods were furious about consolidation, believing that competition kept rates low. In 1901, Morgan and two other railroad owners created the Northern Securities Company to consolidate the operations of the three most important railroads in the region. President Theodore Roosevelt stepped in and ordered his Justice Department to sue the new company under the Sherman Antitrust Act of 1890. The Northern Securities Company was dissolved.

Pierpont Morgan began talks with Charles M. Schwab, president of the Carnegie Company. Morgan wanted to buy Carnegie's steel business and merge it with other steel companies, coal and mining concerns, and shipping firms. Carnegie sold Carnegie Steel to Morgan for $480 million, allowing Morgan to create U.S. Steel, the first billion-dollar company in the world. This vertically integrated company gave Morgan a monopoly on not only the steel business but also every other business that relied on steel. Morgan believed that his company needed to be this large to compete in the steel market with Britain and Germany. In 1903, Schwab broke away and formed Bethlehem Steel.

During the Panic of 1893 (which lasted from 1893 to 1897), fifteen thousand businesses failed, and five hundred banks closed. Unemployment hit unprecedented numbers at 35 percent in New York and 42 percent in Michigan. By 1895, the U.S. Treasury was nearly out of gold: it was the policy to keep gold worth $100 million in the Treasury, and it had dropped to $9 million at its lowest point. Morgan met with President Grover Cleveland and convinced him to allow the Treasury to buy $68 million worth of gold (3.5 million ounces) from the private banks of Morgan and the Rothschilds. The government could pay them back by issuing a thirty-year bond. This act pulled the country out of the slump and tied gold to the U.S. monetary system (known as the gold standard) for years to come.

America experienced another economic contraction in the Panic of 1907. Over twenty thousand banks and trust companies across the country were affected, with no central bank or Federal Reserve to issue guidance.

Trust companies, which handled estates and wills and trust funds, were particularly vulnerable. The 1907 panic exposed many systemic defects. As people hoarded money and banks called in loans, there was no central bank to relieve the monetary stress. Sharp drops in money supply led to severe recessions. The country needed an elastic currency and a permanent lender of last resort. As banks, trust companies, businesses, and the stock market itself began to fail, Morgan brought the country's leading financiers to his New York mansion, where he made them work out a plan to meet the crisis. The U.S. Secretary of the Treasury gave Morgan $35 million to work with. John D. Rockefeller threw in another $10 million. Morgan bought the Tennessee Coal and Iron Company, whose failure was threatening the collapse of the stock market, for $45 million. The presidents of the wealthy trust companies created a $25 million pool to protect the weaker trusts. All of this activity transpired over the course of a week or two.

Historian Frederick Lewis Allen wrote that Pierpont reached the zenith of his influence with the 1907 panic. "Where there had been many principalities, there was now one kingdom, and it was Morgan." Senator Nelson W. Aldrich declared, "Something has got to be done. We may not always have Pierpont Morgan with us to meet a banking crisis." Out of the Panic of 1907 came the Federal Reserve System, where twelve private regional reserve banks would be created and placed under a central political authority that would include the Treasury secretary and presidential appointees.

J. Pierpont Morgan forbade photos of himself without permission. He was self-conscious of his nose, which was becoming deformed by the disease rhinophyma. *Source:* Library of Congress.

J. Pierpont Morgan was larger than life in so many ways. Physically, he was a large man with piercing eyes and a bulbous purple nose. He had suffered from the skin disease acne rosacea since he was a child, and his deformed nose was from rhinophyma, one result of rosacea. As he grew older, his nose deformity got worse, and he hated being photographed. He demanded that all professional photos be retouched, according to historian Jean Strouse. He was fastidious to the details of his appearance, but there was nothing he could do to conceal the disease that was deforming his nose. In spite of this, Morgan carried out numerous extramarital affairs while married to Fanny, who outlived him by a decade.

Morgan's art collection was legendary. After Junius's death, Pierpont's collecting blossomed. He collected books, manuscripts, letters, tapestries, gilded altarpieces, illuminated manuscripts, gold and silver cups, porcelains, ivory, and just about any object he could purchase that was associated with Europe of the past. He owned Napoleon's watch, Leonardo da Vinci's notebooks, Catherine the Great's snuffbox, Medici family jewelry,

The Morgan Library, designed by Charles F. McKim. *Source:* Library of Congress.

Shakespeare's first folios, a five-page letter written by George Washington, and Roman coins. He loved the paintings of old masters. His was the largest collection of any private individual of his day. He wrote to his sister Mary, "I have done with the Greek antiquities. I am at the Egyptian." Pierpont had architect Charles F. McKim design a library for his collection adjacent to his New York home. He filled the Italian Renaissance building with his collections and hired twenty-two-year-old Belle da Costa Greene to catalog them. Belle became famous as the director of the Pierpont Morgan Library. (Morgan also was an important gem collector. His collection was organized by Tiffany's chief gemologist, George Frederick Kunz, and was exhibited at the Paris World's Fair in 1889. The American Museum of Natural History now has the Morgan-Tiffany collection. Morgan also was patron to photographer Edward S. Curtis, giving him $75,000 in 1906 to photograph and produce a series on the American Indian, resulting in a twenty-volume work.)

Morgan owned a series of large yachts over his lifetime. The first was the 165-foot-long, black-hulled steam yacht the *Corsair*. Bought in 1882, Pierpont used it to cruise back and forth to work from his summer home, Cragston, on the west side of the Hudson River near West Point. Morgan used the *Corsair* as a secret meeting place, whether to conduct business or affairs, according to Chernow. After his father's death, Pierpont had *Corsair II* built. It measured over 241 feet in length and was the largest pleasure vessel afloat at that time. In 1898, the navy conscripted *Corsair II* for use in the Spanish-American War. The navy paid $225,000 for the ship, which then became the gunboat *Gloucester*. It was damaged in the Battle of Santiago. Pierpont's *Corsair III* measured three hundred feet at the waterline and required a crew of seventy.

In December of 1912, Morgan was called before the Pujo Committee, a subcommittee of the House Banking and Currency Committee. It was charged with investigating the growing power of bankers and monopolies. The report revealed that at least eighteen different major financial corporations were under the control of a cartel led by three men, including J. P. Morgan. These men, through the resources of seven banks and trust companies, controlled an estimated $2.1 billion. It also reported that

J. Pierpont Morgan and guests at the Columbia Yacht Club. *Source:* Library of Congress.

over $22 billion in resources and capitalization was controlled through 341 directorships (on boards) held in 112 corporations by members of J. P. Morgan's empire. In a book by Louis Brandeis, future Supreme Court Justice, Brandeis compared the $22 billion to the value of all the property in the twenty-two States west of the Mississippi River.

John Pierpont Morgan died just months after the release of the report from the Pujo Commission. The strain of testifying weakened the seventy-five-year-old man, who died four months later in a $500-a-day suite in Rome's Grand Hotel. Historian Chernow thinks this might be overstated. Morgan smoked dozens of cigars a day, ate huge breakfasts, drank to excess, and refused to exercise. He had been sick since childhood and was never really free of illness and depression. The fact that he lived to seventy-five was, instead, a testament to his powerful constitution.

Pierpont's estate, outside of his massive art collection, was valued at $68.3 million (over $1.7 billion in today's dollars). His art collection was valued at $50 million ($1.3 billion). Andrew Carnegie, a fabulously wealthy industrialist, reportedly said, "And to think he was not a rich man." The Morgan family received the bulk of the estate, but over $10 million was given in charitable bequests, including $500,000 to the Cathedral of Saint John the Divine in New York City. The most surprising bequest was that every employee of J. P. Morgan & Company and Morgan Grenfell (the European office) receive money equivalent to a year's salary.

JOHN PIERPONT MORGAN JR.
(1867–1943)

John Pierpont Morgan Jr., known as Jack to the family and close friends, was born to Fanny and John Pierpont Morgan Sr. in 1867. As the first son, he was expected to one day take over the family business. He attended St. Paul's School in New Hampshire and then went on to Harvard, where he graduated in 1889. Jack craved the attention of his father who, because of work and self-absorption, was emotionally and physically unavailable to the boy. Their relationship was formal and stiff. And the delicate, sensitive boy had a tough time finding a place in the world of the famous father. Jack was very attached to his mother, much like his father was to his mother. For forty years, mother and son consoled each other.

Jack met Jane Norton Grew the year he graduated from Harvard. Jessie, as she was called, had a proper Bostonian pedigree, which appealed to Pierpont Morgan, so the two were married in December of 1890. Their marriage made the front page of the *New York Times*.

At age twenty-five, Jack became a partner in the Morgan Banks in New York, Philadelphia, London, and Paris. Pierpont sent Jack and Jessie to London in 1898, where they stayed for eight years. Jack studied banking in the London house of J. S. Morgan & Co. He and Jessie became confirmed Anglophiles—especially Jessie, who found London society much like that in Boston. Earl Grey and Florence Nightingale were their neighbors, and they counted Henry James, Rudyard Kipling, and Sir James Barrie among their acquaintances. Jack bought a three hundred-acre country estate, Wall Hall, that had a turreted house and fake ruins on the grounds, and the fields were stocked with pheasant. While in England, the Morgans had two girls and two boys. The boys were sent to school while the girls were tutored at Wall Hall.

The younger Morgans were received into social circles that would provide them entrée into the world of British nobility and politicians. Jessie was presented to Queen Victoria while Jack trooped about in sword and cocked hat. They befriended Lady Sybil Smith and her husband Vivian Hugh Smith, which got them into Windsor Castle, where Lady Smith's mother, Lady Antrim, was a lady-in-waiting to the queen. As Jack Morgan aged, he began to resemble his father. They were both over six feet tall with broad shoulders, and both sported a mustache. They dressed alike—Jack had his clothes made where Pierpont had his made, and he bought his hats from the same person who made his father's hats. They both avoided the public and, particularly, the press, and were gruff when confronted. Jack, however, did not have his father's complexion problem and protruding nose.

When Pierpont Morgan died in 1913, Jack was thrust into the position of senior partner at J. P. Morgan & Company. He was forty-six years old. His first act was to figure out what to do with his father's massive art collection. He wanted the Metropolitan Museum of Art to build a wing to house the collection, which he would give to them with $1.5 million, but that didn't happen. He knew his father wanted to keep the collection together, but Jack was faced with the prospect of not being able to pay the inheritance taxes of about $3 million and pay the bequests and also have money left over to continue the bank. Jack chose some of the rarest works of art and sold them for $8 million.

Less than two years after the death of Pierpont Morgan, World War I broke out. The British and French governments called upon the Morgan firm to undertake the work of coordinating and purchasing food supplies and munitions in the United States to be sent to Europe. The firm sunk several billion dollars into these purchases. Morgan also organized a syndicate of 2,200 American banks and floated a loan of $500 million of 5 percent bonds guaranteed jointly by Great Britain and France.

During this time, Morgan also survived an assassination attempt at his home when an intruder shot him twice. Erich Muenter, a former German instructor at Harvard, was a pacifist opposed to American arms exports to Europe. He believed that if Morgan withdrew his money in the munitions markets, it would stop the war. Muenter gained entrance to the Morgan's North Shore estate and tried to take the two Morgan daughters hostage. According to police depositions, Jessie Morgan threw herself at Muenter while Jack tried to tackle the man. That's when Morgan took two bullets to the groin. Jack and Jessie managed to get the two pistols from Muenter while Physick, the butler, smashed a chunk of coal over the intruder's head. Muenter committed suicide in Nassau County Jail before the police could determine if he had accomplices.

After the war, Morgan arranged loans to Great Britain, France, Belgium, Italy, Austria, Switzerland, Japan, Argentina, Australia, Cuba, Canada, and Germany. Morgan and his associates issued about $4 billion-worth of domestic bonds in the postwar decade, according to Morgan's obituary in the *New York Times*.

Jessie and Jack Morgan spent about half of their time in England, where they owned a couple of properties. The Morgans held great hunting parties at Wall Hall and on grouse moors in Scotland that they rented for the season. Jack gave the London house that once belonged to his father to the American government to serve as the ambassador's residence. (It's where the Kennedy clan—including the brothers Jack, Bobby, and Teddy—lived when Joseph Kennedy was ambassador to the Court of St. James.) In the summer of 1925, Jessie Morgan fell ill with an inflammation of the brain that put her into a coma for a couple of months. She seemed to be recovering, when she suddenly died. Jack was completely heartbroken. Jessie had proved to be the perfect partner for Morgan, and now she was gone. Morgan didn't remarry and remained a lonely man who never really recuperated from his wife's death.

Prior to the stock market crash of October 1929, Morgan's firm and five other leading banking institutions formed a pool with $240 million, which they fed into the market in an attempt to maintain orderly trading conditions in the Stock Exchange. J. P. Morgan & Co. lost 40 percent of its asset value between 1929 and 1933.

A Senate investigation in 1933 revealed that the Morgan company offered new stock issues to persons on selected lists at prices lower than market quotations. Some of the country's leading citizens were on this list. Morgan explained that none of the stock bargains were offered to people who were currently holding public office. "We never had any occasion to ask favors from legislators or persons in public office, nor have we ever done so," said Morgan.

An avid collector, like his father, Jack Morgan began selling some of his rare paintings and miniatures in 1935. He explained that he wanted to protect his heirs from "buying them back from the government" after his death and that he wanted to leave his estate in a "manageable" condition.

Jack Morgan suffered his first of several heart attacks in 1936. Although he declared that he recovered completely and was in perfect health, he began to have subordinates deal with more of the business details. In the spring of 1937, he went to England to attend the coronation of King George VI and Queen Elizabeth, who were old friends, but was again sidelined by another heart attack.

A yachtsman like his father, Jack Morgan had the *Corsair IV* built in Bath, Maine, for the tidy sum of $2,500,000. It was the largest private yacht constructed up to that time. When it was clear that Great Britain was going to be pulled into World War II, Morgan sold it to the British government for one dollar.

In March 1943, Jack Morgan headed to Florida for a fishing trip in the Gulf of Mexico. While on the train, he suffered a cerebral stroke. He survived less than two weeks and died on March 13, 1943. Morgan was seventy-five, the same age his father had been when he died. The news was not made public until after the closing of the stock market that day so as to not disturb share prices. The *New York Times*, which ran an obituary that began on page one, called him the "last financial titan"—which is what they had also called Pierpont when he died thirty years earlier.

Under Jack's leadership, the House of Morgan became an international powerhouse, and the bank's offices at 23 Wall Street became the gathering place for the world's financial elite. Jack Morgan also knew how to delegate power under his reputable stewardship, which left the bank free of internal squabbling. However, to the public, he was a mystery. Out of step with the twentieth century, he was an anachronistic man who would have been more comfortable in the Victorian era.

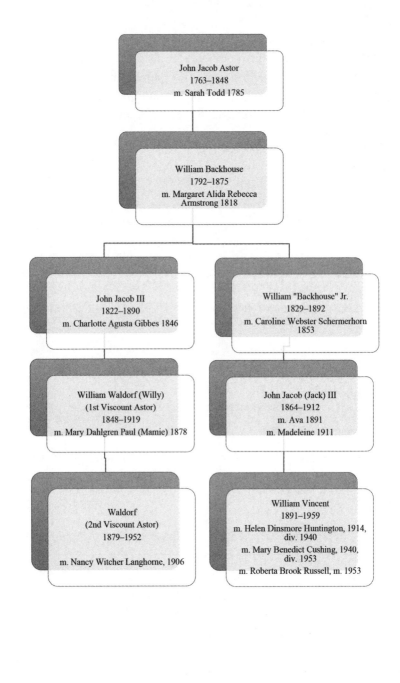

John Jacob Astor
1763–1848
m. Sarah Todd 1785

William Backhouse
1792–1875
m. Margaret Alida Rebecca
Armstrong 1818

John Jacob III
1822–1890
m. Charlotte Agusta Gibbes 1846

William "Backhouse" Jr.
1829–1892
m. Caroline Webster Schermerhorn
1853

William Waldorf (Willy)
(1st Viscount Astor)
1848–1919
m. Mary Dahlgren Paul (Mamie) 1878

John Jacob (Jack) III
1864–1912
m. Ava 1891
m. Madeleine 1911

Waldorf
(2nd Viscount Astor)
1879–1952

m. Nancy Witcher Langhorne, 1906

William Vincent
1891–1959
m. Helen Dinsmore Huntington, 1914,
div. 1940
m. Mary Benedict Cushing, 1940,
div. 1953
m. Roberta Brook Russell, m. 1953

8

Astor

Furs to the Gilded Age

Always take the trick. When the opportunity you seek is before you, seize it. Do not wait until tomorrow on the supposition that your chance will become better, for you may never see it again.

—John Jacob Astor III

The Astor family was one of the fabulously rich American families that captured the public's imagination in the nineteenth and twentieth centuries. The family fortune lay in investing and real estate development. The Astors became the arbiters of New York's wealth and society during the Gilded Age.

John Jacob Astor
(1763–1848)

The family patriarch, John Jacob Astor, was the son of a butcher in the town of Walldorf, Germany. Like his older brothers, he knew he did not want to be a butcher, so at age sixteen, he made his way to London, where his brother George, who worked in a shop selling musical instruments, lived. After a couple of years, John Jacob packed up seven finely crafted flutes and several other items and made his way to New York City, just after the end of the American Revolution. According to historian Peter Stark, Astor heard about the fur trading business from a fellow passenger. He learned that, with an investment of just a few trinkets to trade for pelts with the Indians, a fellow could make a lot of money, particularly if he had contacts in London. Astor tucked this information in the back of his mind.

John Jacob Astor, the patriarch.
Source: Library of Congress.

In New York, John Jacob took a room in a boarding house and soon married Sarah Todd, the daughter of the proprietor. They lived in one room and set up another as a shop for selling fine musical instruments and wild-animal pelts. At first, Astor picked up furs from travelers coming to New York, which he'd then bundle up to take to London, where he found he could make a lot of money selling them. He'd purchase instruments while in England and bring them back to the States to sell.

Soon Astor left his growing family—with Sarah's blessing—and began traveling to upstate New York to visit the Iroquois tribes. He learned how to barter for furs of fox, lynx, bear, mink, beaver, and wolf. He wandered farther afield into the interior of Canada, where Canada's North West Company employed fur traders. Astor bought pelts in volume, taking them back to New York, then sending them to European capitals, where they would fetch staggering prices. In his far-flung journeys, Astor became entranced by the vastness of the wilderness that lay to the west.

By 1800, John Jacob Astor had made almost a quarter of a million dollars (in 1800 dollars), an enormous sum of money, most of it made from selling furs. In addition to selling in Europe, Astor traded in furs, tea, and sandalwood in China. After the successful Lewis and Clark Expedition to the Pacific Northwest, Astor wrote to President Thomas Jefferson to seek permission to establish the American Fur Company to control fur trading from the Great Lakes region to the Columbia River. Astor financed the Astor Expedition of 1810–1812. One group traveled by sea around Cape Horn, and the other went overland. Both hoped to find a practical route to the Pacific Northwest. Their goal was to meet at the mouth of the Columbia River and construct the first American colony on the West Coast. The Columbia River trading post, Fort Astoria, was established in 1811. Astoria would provide the jumping-off point for trade to China—packets of fur would go west and porcelain, silk, and tea would come back.

Members of the overland Astor Expedition discovered South Pass, in present-day Wyoming, which became an important way to get through the Rocky Mountains. South Pass became part of the Oregon, Mormon, and California Trails—the route hundreds of thousands of pioneers would take on their way west in the mid-nineteenth century.

The war with the British in 1812 put a halt to Astor's fur trading when the British captured his trading posts. In 1816 Congress passed a law banning foreign fur traders from the States, partly as a way to punish the British. This enormously benefitted Astor, who bought up most of the Canadian fur-trading companies. Astor's American Fur Company thrived around the Great Lakes, bringing more wealth to the New Yorker. John Jacob Astor commissioned writer Washington Irving (best known for writing the short stories "Rip Van Winkle" and "The Legend of Sleepy Hollow") to pen a history of the Astor Expedition using diaries, documents, and letters supplied by Astor. Irving was also able to interview many of the participants. Called *Astoria: Or, Enterprise Beyond the Rocky Mountains*, it was published in 1836.

By the third decade of the nineteenth century, Astor had ships trading all over the globe. They traded furs and dry goods, silks and tea. Anything of commercial value, Astor traded. In 1816 his American Fur Trading Company bought ten tons of Turkish opium that the company then smuggled into Canton, China, according to historian Peter Stark. Soon, however, Astor sold opium only to Great Britain. (Over the centuries, opium had become such a problem in China that imports of opium were banned in 1799, and then again in 1810. However, the ban had little effect. Opium was also imported to the United States and England.)

As soon as he was able, John Jacob Astor began buying real estate in Manhattan. When he first moved to New York City in the early 1780s, it was a town of about twenty-five thousand. By 1850, the population was over half a million. At the turn of the nineteenth century, Astor began buying tracts of land that lay beyond the city limits. He bought farms and open fields and land along the waterfronts. By 1830, Astor began to focus exclusively on real estate, correctly predicting the rapid buildup of the city. He didn't normally develop the land himself but instead leased it and let others worry about the building.

Astor did, however, build two significant buildings; one was a country house called Hellgate, overlooking the East River at what is today 88th Street. That part of the East River and its estuary was called Hell Gate because of swirling currents. It was here that Astor and Washington Irving met to talk about *Astoria*. The second was a hotel called Astor House, which cost $400,000 to build and opened in 1836. Six stories high with a Greek Revival granite portico opening onto Broadway, Astor House contained three hundred rooms and employed a staff of over one hundred. The ground floor contained shops where you could buy anything from wigs and clocks to pianos and trusses. The dining room was immense, and the silver and china alone cost $20,000. A French chef presided over the kitchen of twelve cooks and sixty waiters. The room rate was two dollars per night, and as editor James Gordon Bennett told his *New York Herald* staff, "Anyone who can pay two dollars a day for a room must be important." When Davy Crockett stayed at the hotel, he reportedly said, assuming that the fur business had paid for it, "Lord help the poor bears and beavers." Astor leased the hotel to Frederick and Simeon Boyden, who had experience running Boston's Tremont House. The Boydens convinced Astor to install seventeen bathing rooms instead of ten. At Astor's death, the Astor House was recognized as one of the best hotels in the world.

When he died in 1848, Astor left an estate worth about $20 million, which would be equivalent to more than $649 million in 2019 dollars. He was the wealthiest person in the United States. On his deathbed, he was quoted as saying: "If I could begin life again knowing what I now know and had money to invest, I would buy every foot of land on the island of Manhattan." His wife, Sarah, predeceased him in 1834. He and Sarah had eight children, but only five lived to adulthood. His firstborn son, John Jacob Astor Jr., was mentally unstable, and his father did not want to make him his heir. This meant the bulk of his estate was left to the second son, William Backhouse Astor Sr. Astor also left $400,000 for a public library, $50,000 for a poorhouse and orphanage in Walldorf, Germany, and enough money to provide care for his oldest son for the rest of his life. Not known for his philanthropic impulses, Astor did, however, support ornithologist and bird artist John James Audubon and the presidential campaign of Henry Clay.

WILLIAM BACKHOUSE ASTOR SR.
(1792–1875)

When John Jacob Astor died, his son William became the richest man in America. Already fifty-six years old when his father died, William had spent his life furthering his father's financial interests.

Born at the end of the eighteenth century, young William was six when the family moved to Broadway in New York. He was educated in a public school until university, when his father sent him to the University of Heidelberg in Germany. It was there that William developed his life-long love of history. He came back to New York and entered into business with his father.

According to William's obituary in the *New York Times*, he understood the minutest details of real estate and building operations. This skill led him to anticipate which parts of New York would grow the fastest and profit the investor handsomely. He knew every building the company owned and leased, even when they ran into the hundreds. When William received $20 million at his father's death, he doubled the amount put toward a public library for the city and became an avid patron for the rest of his life.

Quiet and self-contained, according to the *New York Times*, "in popular belief [he] was only a money-bag." To his friends, however, William Sr. displayed his interests in history and in ancient cultures.

In 1818 he married Margaret Alida Rebecca Armstrong, known as Alida, the daughter of General Armstrong, secretary of war under President Madison. Together they had seven children, three of whom were boys (John, William Jr., and Henry).

THE GRANDCHILDREN OF JOHN JACOB ASTOR SR.

John Jacob Astor III and William Backhouse Astor Jr. were the sons of William Backhouse Astor Sr. and grandsons of John Jacob Astor. There was also a third son, Henry, whom history seems to have forgotten after he married a farmer's daughter in the Hudson Valley near Rhinebeck, New York. This "inappropriate" marriage left Henry on the outs with his father, and he was subsequently left out of his father's will, as were his offspring.

John J. III studied at the University of Gottingen, Columbia, and Harvard Law School. An Episcopalian and a Republican, John J. III had no interest in public service, as seen when he turned down President Rutherford Hayes's offer of the position of minister to England. According to Justin Kaplan, Astor's credo, which he passed on to his son, was "Work hard, but never work after dinner" and "Always take the trick. When the opportunity you seek is before you, seize it. Do not wait until tomorrow on the supposition that your chance will become better, for you may never see it again."

William B. Jr. lived on Fifth Avenue in the mansion next door to his brother John III. William B. Jr. was viewed by his brother, who was seven years his senior, as shiftless and a wastrel. When William B. Jr. graduated from Columbia, he spent his time yachting, raising racehorses (Vagrant, one of his horses, won the Kentucky Derby in 1876), and drinking. According to a contemporary, he was a "one-man temperance society, dedicated to destroying all spirituous liquor even if he had to drink it all himself." He had no interest in business, preferring to sail his boat the *Ambassadress*, the largest private yacht in the world.

John J. III married Charlotte Augusta Gibbes, a deeply religious woman, in 1846. They had one child, William Waldorf Astor, two years later. John J. III built a mansion at 350 Fifth Avenue, a vacation home in Newport, Rhode Island, and a country estate on the Hudson River. He donated money and objects to the Metropolitan Museum of Art and deeded three building lots to the Astor Library (which would later become the New York Public Library), to which he later donated his collection of rare manuscripts. John J. III and Charlotte gave money to the Children's Aid Society and the New York Cancer Hospital. He made some bequests upon his death totaling about $3 million, but given that he left a fortune of $150 million, his gifts only represented .02 percent of his wealth.

William B. Jr. married Caroline Webster "Lina" Schermerhorn in 1853. They had four daughters and one son, John Jacob Astor IV. In addition to his mansion in Manhattan, William B. Jr. had a large estate called Ferncliff, built at Barrytown, New York, along the Hudson River. Today William B. Jr. would be viewed as a bit of a playboy. He had no interest in increasing his financial estate. Instead, he was intent on spending it. He spent many winters in Jacksonville, Florida, where he built several buildings and founded the Florida Yacht Club (even though he had the only yacht in the state). In 1874, he bought 80,000 acres of land north of Orlando, Florida, where he and two partners laid out a 12,000-acre town and called it Manhattan. They built a nondenominational church and a schoolhouse. The Astor Hotel was built right on the St. Johns River and included a steamboat landing. The town was renamed "Astor" in 1884.

Several books have been written about William B. Jr.'s wife, Lina. She was formidable and set herself up as New York's reigning hostess. She developed the concept of New York's Four Hundred, which defined the limits of New York high society. As her friend and bon vivant Ward McAllister said, "If you go outside that number you strike people who are either not at ease in a ballroom or else make other people not at ease." Those lucky enough to be on the list were invited to every party. Some say that Lina came up with the number *four hundred* because that was the number of people who could fit in her ballroom, although others say her ballroom could hold many more than four hundred. Although the list was a bit elastic, it all came down to money, and who was "old money" and who was "new money." Astors considered themselves old money because their wealth began with John Jacob Astor in the late eighteenth century. The Vanderbilts, on the other hand, would be considered new money because Commodore Vanderbilt made his money a generation after John Jacob Astor. The Four Hundred were like characters out of an Edith Wharton novel—mannered and exclusive.

When her sister-in-law Charlotte, John J. III's wife, died in 1887, Lina Astor insisted on being called "Mrs. Astor." As in "the only Mrs. Astor." All mail was to be addressed to her this way, whether she was in New York or at her home in Newport, Rhode Island (where there was more than one Mrs. Astor, which caused endless confusion for the post office). When Mrs. Astor gave a party, the *New York Times* published the guest lists and menus. Midnight suppers might include "terrapin, fillet of beef, canvasback duck, partridge with truffles, quail, game, and foie gras in aspic" all served on silver and gold plates. One of her parties cost $100,000 at a time when the average wage of a skilled worker working ten hours a day and six days a week was less than $700 per year.

At Mrs. Astor's last formal reception in 1905 (she died in 1908), it was reported that she wore a "massive tiara that seemed a burden upon her head, and she was further weighed down by an enormous dog collar of pearls with diamond pendant attachments. She also wore a celebrated Marie Antoinette stomacher of diamonds and a large diamond corsage ornament. Diamonds and pearls were pinned here and there about the bodice. She was a dozen Tiffany cases personified."

William B. Jr. tried to stay as far away as possible from his wife's galas and dinner parties. He could usually be found in Europe or Florida or, later in his life, on the *Nourmahal*, the 250-foot all-steel yacht he had built to replace the *Ambassadress*. *Nourmahal*, which means "Light of the Harem," was William B. Jr.'s pleasure craft. Once, when Mrs. Astor was asked about her husband's absences, she replied, "Oh, he is having a delightful cruise. The sea air is so good for him. It is a great pity I am such a bad sailor, for I should so enjoy accompanying him. As it is, I have never even set foot on the yacht."

John J. III died of heart disease in 1890, two years after his wife died. His son William Waldorf Astor was his only heir and was to inherit about $150 million. Much of John J. III's wealth derived from his inheritance after his father's death, as well as the rent money from squalid tenements he owned, in which three-quarters of New York City's population lived, according to Kaplan.

William B. Jr. died of a ruptured aneurysm while in Paris in 1892. According to the *New York Times* obituary, "The interest that attached to

William Astor was due in this country to his wealth rather than to his personality. He lacked the democratic ways of his elder brother and was by no means a familiar figure in this city of late years. Having come into an abundant fortune at this father's death, he preferred to pass his time abroad rather than in the country and for years he spent the greater part of his life in Europe or in cruising about in his steam yacht *Nourmahal*, a vessel fit for any sea and having generally the equipment of an ocean steamship." His wife, Caroline, outlived him by sixteen years. The heir to William Jr.'s wealth was John Jacob Astor IV.

WILLIAM WALDORF ASTOR (1848–1919) AND JOHN JACOB ASTOR IV (1864–1912)

The two cousins, William "Willy" Waldorf Astor and John "Jack" Jacob Astor IV, engaged in a kind of one-upmanship for their entire lives. Although sixteen years apart in age, they grew up in adjacent mansions on Fifth Avenue in New York.

Willy was the only child of John Jacob Astor III and Charlotte Astor and grew up in a religious, dour household. Willy once said in an interview, "I was myself brought up severely and kept upon a pitiful allowance. I lived in an atmosphere of sinister religion filled with hobgoblins. . . . The hellfire sermons of my childhood, the like of which no congregation out of Scotland would listen to today, frightened me silly, and I knew those red hot things were being made ready for me." He was brought up by governesses and attended Columbia Grammar School, the University of Gottingen (where his father had studied), and then Columbia Law. While in Europe, he took the opportunity to visit Italy, where he engaged in what he called "a love adventure . . . with a young lady of rare charm." He was recalled to the States by his parents, who were likely horrified about his Italian liaison. However, Willy stayed in touch with the woman until her death in 1909.

A romantic at heart and lover of history and art, Willy developed a passion for Renaissance art and classical antiquities, something he would collect later in his life. He also had an artistic side and dabbled in sculpture, drawing, and painting. His art was relegated to the background after graduating with a law degree and entering the family business, where he excelled in real estate law. When Willy was thirty, he married Mary

"Mamie" Dahlgren Paul (1858–1894) of Philadelphia, and they went on to have five children, with three living to adulthood.

Willy briefly became a politician, an unlikely career for someone of his social class. He was elected to the New York State Assembly in 1878 and the New York State Senate in 1880 and 1881. Then he was defeated in a run for the U.S. Congress in 1881. President Chester A. Arthur appointed him minister to Italy in 1882, which was a welcome respite from the dirty world of politics. He and Mamie lived in an enormous residence in Rome, and they entered Roman society. Mamie became a court favorite whom Queen Margharita named the "most beautiful woman in Italy." Willy threw himself into all things Italian—studying sculpture, drawing, and Italian history. He began to collect Italian artifacts and art on a grand scale.

After the death of his mother in 1887 and his father in 1890, Willy decided to put his "English Plan" into action—a decision that his family would fare better in another land. So they moved, with Willy issuing the parting thoughts that "America is not a fit place for a gentleman to live. [It is] good enough for any man who has to make a livelihood, though why traveled people of independent means should remain there more than a week is not readily to be comprehended."

John Jacob Astor IV, known as Jack, grew up the pampered boy of his four older sisters and his mother, Caroline. His father, William B. Jr., was rarely home. Jack went to prep school at St. Paul's in Concord, New Hampshire, and then wound up at Harvard for three years, where he left without earning a degree. After several years of dilettantish behavior, he received the sobriquet "Jack-Ass" in the press.

At age twenty-six, much to his mother, Lina's, relief, Jack married Ava Lowle Willing of Philadelphia. "She rides well," the *New York Times* reported, "dances beautifully, is musical, quite literary and uncommonly intelligent." The Astors gave the bride and groom a furnished house on Fifth Avenue and diamonds from Lina's collection. Jack and Ava had a son, William Vincent, in 1891, and then Ava proceeded to live her own life, making no attempt to hide her disdain for her husband. She persuaded Jack to have architect Stanford White design an athletic complex at Ferncliff, the Astor estate near Rhinebeck, New York. It contained a tennis court, two squash courts, a marble swimming pool, a bowling alley, a billiard room, and a rifle range. Jack had a laboratory built at Ferncliff so he could tinker and get out of the way of his self-indulgent, sharp-tongued wife.

Jack spent most of his time with their son Vincent (as the boy preferred to be called), whom he adored and who adored him. Ava called the boy "stupid and avoided him because he was clumsy and lumpish looking, had big feet, and, perhaps worst of all, reminded her of his father."

The Astor cousins—Willy and Jack—were worth about $200 million in 1890. Right after his father died, Willy tore down the house he had grown up in to make way for the construction of a new hotel. His Aunt Caroline's house—directly next door and the scene of Lina's noteworthy suppers and balls for the Four Hundred—was to be rendered almost uninhabitable by the excavation, dirt, and noise. When the Waldorf Hotel was built, his Aunt Caroline could look out onto an eleven-story brick wall right next to her house. Jack, in response, built a four-story, French Renaissance chateau-style, $2 million double home, further up Fifth Avenue, for his mother and his own family. Designed by Richard Morris Hunt, the same man who designed homes for the Vanderbilts, it contained the city's largest private ballroom.

Ava Astor, first wife of John Jacob "Jack" Astor IV. *Source:* Library of Congress.

When the Waldorf Hotel was finished in 1893, it was the most luxurious hotel in the country. It contained several private restaurants, including the Palm Garden, the most exclusive and expensive eating place in the city, where the waiters had to speak French and German as well as English. The opening of the Waldorf was a lavish affair and was the lead story on page one of the *New York Times* the following day, which called it a "brilliant social event." Willy, who by this time was living in England with his family, came to see the Waldorf just once.

Jack, who was still furious about the hotel's intrusion on his mother's life, threatened to tear down his mother's house and replace it with a row of horse stables. However, when Jack learned that the Waldorf grossed $4 million the first year, he decided to build a bigger and better hotel right next to the Waldorf. It was several stories taller, and although built in the same style as the Waldorf, the Astoria, as it was called, was much larger. When it opened in 1897, George C. Boldt, the Astoria's proprietor (what we would call the *general manager* today), convinced the cousins that they would make more money if they combined forces. So a three hundred-foot marble corridor connected the two buildings, as did the hyphenated name, the Waldorf-Astoria. (This is not the Waldorf-Astoria Hotel we know today. The Astors' Waldorf-Astoria hotel was razed in 1929 to make way for the Empire State Building. When the new Waldorf-Astoria was built on Park Avenue in 1931, the Astors didn't build it. The owners of the new hotel bought the right to use the name for one dollar.)

Willy and his family were firmly ensconced in British life. In 1899 he renounced his American citizenship and became a British citizen, swearing allegiance to Queen Victoria. He became known as William the Traitor in some American circles. To the British, he was viewed as an American invader. One London journal complained, "If this sort of thing is allowed to go on, we shall soon be governed, not by Downing Street, but by Wall Street."

William bought property in London and in the countryside. His grandest acquisition was Cliveden, a 376-acre estate on the Upper Thames, bought from the Duke of Westminster for $1.25 million. The main house was built in 1666 by the Duke of Buckingham. Queen Victoria, who had visited eight times, wrote in her journal, "It is a perfection of a place. First of all the view is so beautiful, & then the house is a bijou of taste." Willy redid the house and gardens to his taste and then surrounded the whole thing with a high wall topped with broken glass. Cliveden had been open to the public for a century before William bought the estate. Now people couldn't even catch a glimpse of the house because William replaced the iron grille that closed across the drive with a solid-wood gate. A cartoonist in a London newspaper renamed Cliveden "Walled-off Astoria" and showed its owner as a strutting eagle, a British flag tied to his tail, standing on a ground covered with bags of dollars.

The original Waldorf-Astoria Hotel in New York City. *Source:* Library of Congress.

In 1906, William bought Hever Castle, a manor house in Kent and the childhood home of Anne Boleyn, second wife of Henry VIII. Astor spent $10 million renovating Hever to what he believed the place had looked like four hundred years earlier, including installing a moat and a drawbridge. Again, he was ridiculed in the English press.

Meanwhile, when the prospect of a war with Spain over the destiny of Cuba resulted in the destruction of the battleship *Maine* in Havana

Harbor in 1898, Jack Astor was desperate to go to war. He got a commission as an army inspector general with the rank of lieutenant colonel. Astor lent the navy his 250-foot yacht *Nourmahal* and offered free passage for troops and volunteers on the Illinois Central Railroad, which he owned. He also created, financed, and outfitted his own regiment, the Astor Brigade. Jack went to Cuba for a month and was known as "Colonel Astor" for the rest of his life.

The two cousins continued the hotel battles in New York. First, one cousin would build a hotel, and then the other would respond by building his own. In this way, New York City became the home to the Regis, the New Netherland, the Astor, and the Hotel Knickerbocker. Between the two of them, they built six hotels, and in so doing found themselves the city's premier innkeepers. They also virtually invented the American luxury hotel. As historian Kaplan points out, "They had chosen hotels to be the stage for a family drama of pride, spite, rivalry, self-projection, and the love of grandeur and prominence."

Finally, in 1908 Mrs. Astor died. Once the doyenne of high society, Caroline Astor died at the age of seventy-eight, and with her went her rigid notions of high society. This freed her son Jack and his estranged wife, Ava, to obtain a divorce. By that time, the couple had two children, Vincent, age eighteen, and Alice, age six. Ava got custody of Alice and an annual allowance of $50,000, plus a hefty settlement. Jack took the opportunity to redo the white marble house on Fifth Avenue completely. Then he reentered the social scene at age forty-four.

Two years later, in 1910, Jack was frequently seen in the company of Madeleine Talmage Force, a recent debutante and graduate of Miss Spence's School for Girls. Madelaine was seventeen, a year younger than Jack's son Vincent. Soon the couple was inseparable. They married in 1911 when Madeleine turned eighteen and Jack was forty-six. They took a long leisurely trip along the Nile, staying on a houseboat; then, when it was time to return to New York, they booked passage on the maiden voyage of the newest and grandest ship afloat, the *Titanic*.

Madelaine, who was five months pregnant, managed to get into a lifeboat as the unsinkable ship began sinking after striking an iceberg in the cold North Atlantic. Jack helped another woman and her daughter into the last couple of seats. As the boat was being lowered into the sea, Jack called out to Madeleine to not be afraid, for the seas were calm. Then he said he'd see her in the morning. That was the last time they saw each other. Of the 1,517 passengers and crew who died in the sinking, only 333 bodies were recovered, including Jack's. His body was retrieved, a week later, because he was wearing a life jacket. They found his gold pocket watch (which his son Vincent wore for the rest of his life) and over $2,500 in his pocket. Madelaine and Jack's baby was born four months later and was named John Jacob "Jakey" Astor VI.

Seven years later, in 1919, Jack's cousin Willy died of heart disease while in England. Two years before his death, Willy got what he wanted: He rose to the peerage, becoming first a Baron in 1916 and then a Viscount in 1917.

Vincent received $65 million upon his father's death on the *Titanic*. Three million dollars was left in trust for Alice and $10 million for Jakey. Vincent would marry three times. His third wife was Brooke Astor, the reigning socialite of New York for decades. She, unlike the other Astors, gave most of her Astor money away to organizations in New York City through a philanthropic foundation she set up after Vincent's death in 1959. Brooke Astor died at the age of 105 in 2007.

Jack Astor, around the time he married Madeleine. He would soon die on the *Titanic*. *Source:* Library of Congress.

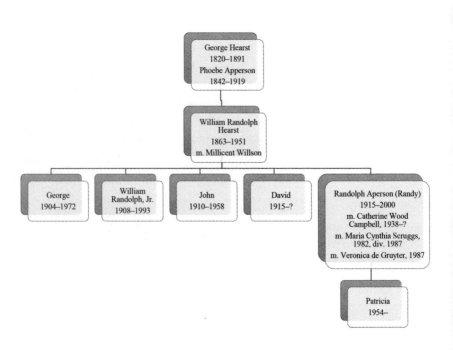

9

Hearst

The Newspaper Business

These young people are all mad as March Hares on the money question and seem to think there is no limit to the bankroll . . . all work and no play may make Jim a dull boy, but no work and all play makes Jim all kinds of a jackass. I want you to get our youngsters together and tell them I am going to shut down on the money supply.

—WILLIAM RANDOLPH HEARST,
IN A LETTER TO HIS WIFE MILLICENT

IN MANY WAYS, THE HISTORY OF THE HEARST DYNASTY FOLLOWS A classic trajectory—the first generation makes the money, then succeeding generations do their best to spend the money. However, because of the way William Randolph Hearst structured his will, today the privately held Hearst Corporation has made the Hearst family one of the wealthiest families in America.

GEORGE HEARST
(1820–1891)
The story of George Hearst is the story of a self-made man and the kind of story many of us imagine when we think of the nineteenth-century history of the American West. Born in rural Franklin County, Missouri, Hearst was one of three children raised on a family farm. His father, William Hearst, raised produce with the help of African American slaves, which was then sold in his own general store. (Although Missouri did not secede from the Union in the prelude to the Civil War, it was a hotly contested state, and soldiers from Missouri fought as both Union and Confederate soldiers during the war.)

George Hearst had very little public schooling outside of learning rudimentary arithmetic and reading, but as is seen in the trajectory of his life, he managed to become a multimillionaire and United States senator. He was, however, always interested in mining and spent much of his childhood visiting local mines and learning about their operations.

In 1850, after hearing about the discovery of gold at Sutter's Mill in California in 1848, he set out for the West, joining a rush of hopeful prospectors, eventually numbering in the hundreds of thousands. President James K. Polk announced in his inaugural address: "The accounts of the abundance of gold are of such an extraordinary character as would scarcely command belief were they not corroborated by the authentic reports of officers in the public service." By the time Hearst reached California, panning for gold in a river or stream had played out and was not yielding results, so miners turned to hydraulic mining—directing jets of water under very high pressure at gold-bearing gravel deposits. Hydraulic mining led to widespread environmental devastation of the landscape. By the mid-1880s, it's estimated that eleven million ounces of gold, worth about $7.5 billion in today's prices, had been recovered during the California Gold Rush.

George Hearst made a decent living as a prospector in California, especially when he diversified and opened a general store. In 1859, Hearst heard about a silver find in western Utah territory. He managed to buy a one-sixth interest in the Ophir Mine—part of what would become known as the Comstock Lode—and the first year, Hearst and his partners sent thirty-eight tons of high-grade silver ore back to California to be smelted in San Francisco. They made over $2 million (today's dollars) in profit. Hearst plowed his money back into mining and some real estate holdings in San Francisco.

In 1860, forty-year-old Hearst returned to Missouri. Both of his siblings were dead, and his father had died before Hearst left for California. Now his mother was not in good health and needed his help. She died of tuberculosis six months later. While in Missouri, he met local schoolteacher Phoebe Apperson. She was eighteen. She was small and, according to historian Alexandra Nickliss, people perceived her as physically frail because of her slight build. George Hearst stood almost a foot taller than Phoebe, with a rough face, deep-set blue eyes, and a bushy, long beard. He was unsophisticated and was sometimes described as loud, crude, and flamboyant. He was illiterate but not ignorant. And he was stubborn. Two years later, they married and moved to San Francisco, California, traveling by ship from New York to the Isthmus of Panama, which they crossed by rail and then sailed up the west coast of Mexico to San Francisco. In 1863, they had their only child, William Randolph Hearst.

George Hearst often left Phoebe and their young son alone for much of Will's childhood. George and Phoebe would essentially begin to lead separate lives. Hearst had become an expert on mining in the West and was called in as a consultant to assess the value of prospective mining ventures. He also continued to sink money into mines, including the Ontario Mine in Utah and, most famously, the Homestake Mine in the Black Hills of South Dakota. The Homestake Mining Operation became the leading producer of gold in the United States. Hearst also bought a quarter interest in the Anaconda Mine in Butte, Montana, which became the world's largest and most profitable copper mine.

In 1878, Hearst began developing the massive Piedra Blanca Ranch in southern California that he had purchased in 1865. The site would later become home to San Simeon—the Hearst Castle—built by his son, William.

In 1865 George was nominated by the Democrats to serve in the California Assembly, where he was, naturally, appointed to the Committee of Mines and Mining Interests. He was gone for much of the 1865–1866 term. Hearst was always interested in politics, and in 1880 he bought the small daily newspaper the *San Francisco Examiner* because he knew that this would be a powerful political tool for promoting his candidates and his own candidacy for office, according to historian David Nasaw. In 1884 George pushed for the election of Grover Cleveland to the presidency, hoping that when the Democrat got into office, he would be chosen to be a senator from California. Unfortunately, California went Republican, so Hearst would have to wait. His chance came in 1886 when the U.S. senator representing California died while in office. The Democratic governor of California appointed Hearst to take the late senator's seat, so the Hearsts headed to Washington, D.C. He was duly elected by the legislature later in 1886.

George Hearst, U.S. Senator from California, died while in office in 1891. His wife, Phoebe Apperson Hearst, inherited her husband's wealth of over $157 million in today's dollars.

WILLIAM RANDOLPH HEARST
(1863–1951)

William Randolph Hearst was the only offspring of George and Phoebe Apperson Hearst. Born in San Francisco, his childhood was punctuated by long absences of his father and a doting mother who wanted her son by her side at all times. This resulted in a spotty education for young William (known throughout his life as Will, Bill, W. R., and The Chief). He led a semi-nomadic childhood, traveling with his mother to the East Coast and Europe for months at a time, without regard for formal education. However, Will was a clever boy—well read, able to speak and read German and French, and quite knowledgeable about history and art. Because of his nomadic lifestyle, young Hearst had few childhood friends.

When Hearst was in his late teens, his mother, Phoebe, decided she wanted her son to attend Harvard.

William Randolph Hearst in 1906. *Source:* Library of Congress.

She took Will on one last tour of Europe, bringing along a tutor to prepare him for St. Paul's School in New Hampshire, where he was to spend one miserable year. Phoebe then hired more tutors to prepare Will for the Harvard entrance examinations, which Will passed.

Hearst spent his time at Harvard spending his lavish monthly allowance on dinners, parties, and clothes from New York. He was admitted to

the top social clubs, including Delta Kappa Epsilon (DKE), and his soph-
omore year was elected business manager of the *Harvard Lampoon* (where
he increased the advertising revenue by 300 percent). Historian David
Nasaw writes, "In less than two years . . . he had gotten himself elected to
the top clubs on campus, earned a reputation as a first-class dandy, grown
an impressive mustache, found a splendid tailor, and acquired a pet alliga-
tor named Charlie." The one thing he did not do at Harvard was study.
He was finally asked to leave Harvard, without earning a degree.

While Hearst was in college, his mother often stayed in New York
City and invited her boy to visit over the weekends. Will discovered the
New York World, published by Joseph Pulitzer, which spoke to a decidedly
urban audience. Pulitzer shortened the paper's title to the *World*, which
was unlike the other stuffy or dull papers in the city. The *World* brought
excitement into the readers' lives. And Pulitzer was making money hand
over fist. None of this was lost on Hearst. On the day his father was taking
the oath of office for U.S. senator from California, Will's name appeared
for the first time on the masthead as "Proprietor" of the *San Francisco
Examiner.*

Hearst's time at the head of the *San Francisco Examiner* was a proving
ground for the young publisher. Will brought in the best writers and artists that money could buy, including Mark Twain, Jack London, Ambrose
Bierce, and Homer Davenport. He also outfitted the paper with up-to-
date equipment. In the eight years he was at the helm, William Randolph
Hearst took what was little more than a four-page newsletter and trans-
formed it into a fully formed daily newspaper that took on corruption
within its pages. It soon became San Francisco's dominant paper.

When George Hearst died in 1891, he left everything to his wife,
Phoebe. Will knew that he would inherit it all when his mother died,
but that left him without the kind of money he had grown accustomed
to receiving. He had no money or property of his own. Since his days
at Harvard, Will had a mistress named Tessie Powers, who had been a
waitress in Cambridge. Hearst had paid for her apartment in Cambridge,
and then, when he moved to San Francisco, Tessie made the move as
well. George and Phoebe knew about what they viewed as his "youthful
indiscretion," and Phoebe, in particular, didn't like it one bit. Will and

Tessie traveled and attended functions together, which Phoebe thought was totally inappropriate. After her husband's death, though, Phoebe had the upper hand because she controlled the purse strings. She forced him to give up his relationship with Tessie if he wanted to receive a monthly salary of $2,500.

Caricature of Hearst drawn by cartoonist Homer Davenport in 1896. *Source:* Library of Congress.

In 1895, Hearst bought the *New York Morning Journal* for $150,000 (money given to him for this purpose by Phoebe). This purchase would put him in direct competition with Joseph Pulitzer's *World*. Hearst brought in crackerjack writers like Stephen Crane and then hired all of Pulitzer's Sunday newspaper staff, as well as his creator of the color comics. Hearst paid his employees well and let them chase interesting stories. Soon Hearst and Pulitzer engaged in a circulation war that led both papers to engage in what would become known as "yellow journalism": publishing stories that were less than truthful and were aimed at influencing public opinion. When a war between Cuba and Spain was on the horizon, both Hearst and Pulitzer kept stories on the front page that emphasized Spanish atrocities toward Cubans. When the United States invaded Cuba, Hearst sailed to Cuba as a war correspondent. Hearst and Pulitzer called a truce on their fierce competition after each of their newspapers lost money covering the Spanish-American War.

Joseph Pulitzer and William Randolph Hearst square off in this political cartoon about the Spanish-American War. *Source:* Library of Congress.

In 1903, Hearst married Millicent Veronica Willson, a New York City chorus girl, who at twenty-one, was almost half Will's age. Hearst, who had a great fondness for light musicals that featured showgirls, had been seeing Millicent since she was sixteen. Her father was a dancer in

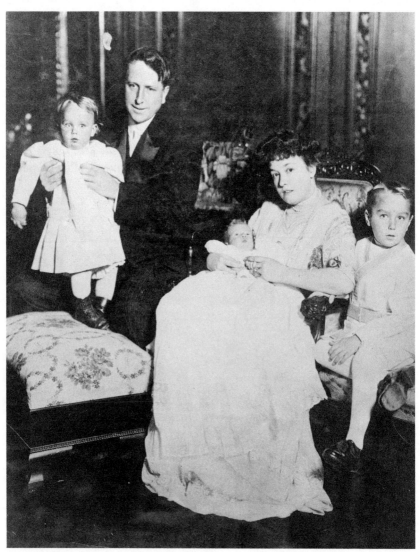

Portrait of the Hearst family in 1915. *Source:* Library of Congress.

vaudeville, and Millicent's older sister was also a chorus girl. They got married in 1903 so Millicent could accompany him to Washington, D.C., where he was about to begin a stint as a congressman. Wishing her son would marry a socialite and not a showgirl, Phoebe was not happy about the union and did not attend the wedding. William Randolph Hearst and Millicent would have five sons: George, William Randolph Jr., John, David, and Randolph.

Always interested in politics, Hearst was twice elected to the United States House of Representatives as a Democrat, serving from 1903 to 1907. Rather than run for reelection to Congress, Hearst made an unsuccessful bid for governor of New York. He also ran for the presidential nomination and twice ran for mayor of New York. He never held another public office outside of his time as a congressman.

Hearst became a publishing magnate in the United States, eventually owning papers across the country, including the *Los Angeles Examiner,* the *Boston American,* the *Washington Herald,* the *Detroit Times,* and the *Seattle Post-Intelligencer.* He bought and became the publisher of magazines such as *Good Housekeeping, Town and Country,* and *Cosmopolitan.* Hearst also owned King Features Syndicate, a film company, and a couple of news services. In addition to reporting on the news, Hearst also made the news. In 1928 he sponsored the first circumnavigation of the world by an airship, the *LZ 127 Graf Zeppelin.* On board was Grace Marguerite, Lady Hay Drummond-Hay, who, in addition to being the first woman to travel around the world by air, wrote a series of articles for Hearst papers.

Hearst was always a profligate spender. Until his mother died, she was in charge of the purse strings, having inherited the bulk of her husband's wealth. Once Hearst began making money from his publishing empire, he began borrowing money from banks instead of going to Phoebe, although he did that as well. He bought whatever he wanted with little regard for how much it cost. Mr. Hearst's lawyer explained the publisher's attitude toward money: "Money as such bores him. His idea of money is that it is something to do something with. He is a builder. He wants to build buildings. He wants to build magazines. He wants to develop ranches. He builds hotels in New York. His idea is to build, build, build all the time. I have said it repeatedly that in his make-up there is just almost a blank space in relation to money." By 1916, he had borrowed nearly $2 million from his mother. (When Phoebe died three years later, Hearst, age fifty-six, inherited $7.5 million.)

In 1915 Hearst met Marion Davies. Marion was a chorus girl, and at the age of eighteen, she was thirty-four years younger than Hearst. By the spring of 1916, they saw each other regularly, at parties, dinners,

Actress and singer Marion Davies. *Source:* Library of Congress.

and gatherings at a suite of rooms Hearst rented near Broadway. He was determined to keep his affair from Millicent and his mother, Phoebe, and embarked on living a double life, according to Nasaw. Marion's career blossomed due to the abundance of favorable publicity she was receiving in Heart's newspapers. By 1921, Millicent and Will were leading almost entirely separate lives. Millicent lived in one of the largest private apartments in New York and ran a huge household of five children and dozens of servants. She took on a prominent role in several charities.

In 1922 Hearst was probably at the height of his fame and power as a newspaper publisher. He owned twenty newspapers in thirteen cities, and he had begun acquiring radio stations and magazines. With his vast media holdings, it's likely that at that time, he was making more money than any publisher ever made. His expenditures were fabulous as well. It is doubtful whether any American citizen ever had lived on so lavish a scale. His 240,000-acre ranch at San Simeon, with its fifty miles of oceanfront, was crowned by a great mansion and three vast guest houses designed by Julia Morgan, all of which were filled with works of art and one of the world's greatest collections of curios. Hearst was an avid collector of just about everything. His *New York Times* obituary stated: "He acquired Etruscan tombs, California mountain ranges, herds of yak, Elizabethan caudle cups, Crusaders' armor, painting, tapestries, a knocked-down and crated Spanish abbey or two, fifteenth-century choir stalls, dozens of Mexican bridles, several Egyptian mummies, and hundreds of other items, many of which he never saw." Hearst owned a castle in Wales and numerous apartments in New York.

Millicent and W. R. stayed married but did not live together after 1927. From that date on, Marion Davies was Hearst's companion, and they lived together as a couple in various properties Hearst owned, mostly in California. Davies starred in a number of movies throughout the twenties and early thirties, and although she was quite good, she never attained the status or star power Hearst thought she deserved.

With the Great Depression came the economic collapse of Hearst's great media empire. "By the mid-thirties, Hearst was so deeply in debt he asked his friend Joseph Kennedy to help him reorganize his companies. Kennedy's accountants discovered that Hearst's corporations owed more

Hearst's Castle: The sprawling San Simeon built by Julia Morgan. *Source:* Library of Congress.

than $80 million and that $58 million of it was secured by Hearst's personal guarantees," according to the *New Yorker*. Forced by the courts to reorganize in 1937, the Hearst Corporation came out of the ashes having shed the newspapers, the film company, and many of William Randolph Hearst's collections of tapestries, art, and silver. Even Marion Davies sold everything and gave Hearst $1 million to satisfy some of his creditors. At age seventy-four, Hearst became an employee of the very company he built.

Davies retired from the movies to spend more time with Hearst. She also began to drink heavily and, despite Hearst's best efforts to limit her access to liquor, she became an alcoholic, according to Nasaw. W. R. lived another fourteen years. For the first decade, Hearst and Davies lived in San Simeon or one of the other houses Hearst owned in California, but for the last four years of his life, they lived in a house in Beverly Hills that would be much more manageable for the elderly man. Hearst suffered from heart problems and was an invalid during those last years. He had gone from being a tall, six-foot-two, two hundred–pound man to a shrunken shadow of himself, at 128 pounds. That, however, did not stop him from writing and then calling his editors to give them orders and advice on how he wanted them to run their newspapers.

Hearst had always run his papers as advocacy newspapers. He was the first major publisher to understand that the "communications media were potentially more powerful than the parties and their politicians . . . he was not interested in reporting the news, but in making it," according to Nasaw. As the twentieth century wore on, papers were moving toward a fair and balanced approach toward journalism. Hearst used his newspapers as a bully pulpit, and unabashedly so. He was an isolationist during the two world wars and became rabidly anti-Roosevelt and anti–New Deal during the 1930s. He advocated making Palestine a Jewish homeland. Hearst went from being progressive to being a right-wing reactionary, which is likely the reason no banks would lend him money in the late 1930s, leading to the bankruptcy of his empire.

In 1941, twenty-five-year-old Orson Welles wrote, directed, and starred in the movie *Citizen Kane*, which was a very thinly disguised movie about William Randolph Hearst. At the center of the film is Charles Foster Kane, a larger-than-life newspaper mogul who is married but falls for a young, struggling singer. Whereas Marion Davies turned out to be a good actress, her film counterpart, Susan Alexander, was a terrible singer who was thrust into larger venues and more difficult performances by Kane. Kane and Alexander retire to a mist-wreathed castle, Xanadu, filled with things collected by Kane. Hearst was furious when he heard about the film and refused to let any of his newspapers mention it. He also managed to get many of his friends who owned chains of movie houses to refuse to show the movie. Although it received rapturous reviews from the critics, it was not that popular with the public. After a year, *Citizen Kane* faded from the public view and was really only revived when it was sold to television. Today, *Citizen Kane* often occupies the top spot among the best films ever made. William Randolph Hearst and Marion Davies refused to see the film.

William Randolph Hearst died on August 14, 1951, at the age of eighty-eight.

THE HEARST BOYS: THE THIRD GENERATION

When William Randolph Hearst died, one stipulation in his will stated that the Hearst Corporation would remain under family control as long as any grandchild survived after his death. A board of trustees controls the family business—five trustees are from the Hearst family, and the other eight are to be chosen from Hearst executives. This prevented the sons from breaking up the empire and selling off the assets.

Like his father, William Randolph Hearst was an absentee father. Bill Jr. recalled, "His silences toward us were often difficult to understand and bear. The only reasonable explanation that I have been able to come to over the years was his far-flung company and other responsibilities. . . . In not spending more time with his wife and children, my father made the biggest mistake of his life. It left an emptiness in all of us."

W. R. interfered in his son's lives from a distance. Randolph Hearst recognized that none of them had the "talent or drive of the old man" and that they all knew it. Although Hearst wanted them to take over the publishing empire he had built, he warned them that "he would not treat us like a rich man's sons. Each of us was told he would have to prove himself to my father's satisfaction."

None of the boys graduated from college, but neither had their father. One by one, as they left school, W. R. apprenticed them to trusted executives in his publishing companies who were to teach them, and watch them, and report back to their father. Bill Jr. wrote in his memoir, "Coming of age was a very disturbing time for each of us. We had been sheltered from many of life's cruelties, despite various warnings by Pop that making a living was no easy business. Most of us felt we needed more time and greater warning from him before facing the problem of a career. The working world came as a cold and perhaps even cruel blast of new air. My brothers felt that Pop treated us harshly."

The sons were put in positions they couldn't handle at very young ages. George, at nineteen, was given a job at the *San Francisco Examiner*. He was fired, given another job, then fired again. After three years of this, he was sent east to serve as president of the *New York American* at age twenty-two. A year later, he was sent back west to take over the *Examiner*. W. R. wrote to George that under his lack of leadership, the *Examiner* was beginning to deteriorate.

Bill Jr. joined the *New York American* as a City Hall reporter at age twenty. He worked his way up until he was named publisher of the *American* while still in his twenties. W. R. complained about Bill's playboy antics, drinking, and love of fast cars. He telegraphed him in 1927, "Please keep out of airplanes, Bill. Am afraid you will break your neck just as you are getting to be useful newspaper man. Am serious about this."

W. R. wrote to his third son John after John had been asked leave UC Berkeley, for failing to attend classes: "Your failure to attend school makes it necessary for me to end your futile attempts at education . . . you will surrender your automobile or sell it, because I will not give you money to take care of it. [You will go to work at a paper in San Francisco immediately]. You will probably be better able to get along on some other paper than any of my papers because I do not want you merely to be a dependent in journalism and be as big a failure in journalism as you have been in your studies." John was only seventeen when W. R. wrote him this letter. John got married and, after a lengthy and expensive honeymoon, went to New York to take a position as president of the Hearst Company, which oversaw *Town & Country*, *Harper's Bazaar*, and a few other magazines. He got a salary of $100,000.

In 1930 W. R. wrote to Millicent saying, "These young people are all mad as March Hares on the money question and seem to think there is no limit to the bankroll . . . all work and no play may make Jim a dull boy, but no work and all play makes Jim all kinds of a jackass. I want you to get our youngsters together and tell them I am going to shut down on the money supply . . . these nincompoops are never satisfied and are being ruined by living far beyond their means and mine. Please read them a lecture and make them keep their expenses down." Oh, the irony. Like father, like sons.

Of all the brothers, Bill Jr. (1908–1993) was probably the son that would come to exemplify the Hearst name in the world of publishing. When he died of a heart attack at age eighty-five, he was the editor in chief of a Hearst media empire that owned daily newspapers, magazines, radio and television stations, a cable television station, two book-publishing companies, and the King Features Syndicate. Bill shared a Pulitzer Prize for international reporting on an eight-part series about the Soviet Union in 1956 and won the Overseas Press Club award two years later. For forty years, he wrote the "Editor's Report" column that ran in all of the Hearst papers. When William Randolph Hearst Jr. took over the Hearst Corporation, he was able to restore a measure of family control.

However, despite all his achievements, Bill wrote, "I lived in my father's shadow all my life."

Although all of the boys would work in the family business, the brother who lived the longest was Randolph Apperson Hearst, "Randy." He attended Harvard and became chairman of the Hearst Corporation from 1973 to 1996. He was serving as editor and president of the *San Francisco Examiner* when Patty, one of his five daughters, was kidnapped by the Symbionese Liberation Army in 1974. He was now a headline in his own newspaper.

Patty was a student at Berkeley when she was taken in by a radical antifascist group that advocated the overthrow of corporations and governments. The Symbionese Liberation Army (SLA) demanded that Hearst feed all the poor people in San Francisco. They demanded a $400 million ransom. Several months after the kidnapping, Patty Hearst was seen toting a gun during a bank robbery. She was eventually apprehended and tried and sentenced to seven years in jail. Patty served almost two years in jail before President Jimmy Carter commuted her sentence to the twenty-two months already served. Bill Clinton officially pardoned her in 2001. She was the leading witness in a trial against SLA members in 2002.

In 2016, the Hearst fortune of $24.5 billion was shared among sixty-seven family members. Today the Hearst Corporation is headed by William R. Hearst III, a grandson of William Randolph Hearst. It owns hundreds of magazines, dozens of newspapers, and stakes in ESPN,

Lifetime, and A&E. Recently, Steven Swartz, the CEO of Hearst Corporation, invested in cable channel Vice TV and the medical software firm MedHOK. According to *Forbes*, in 2016 the Hearsts were the ninth wealthiest family in America.

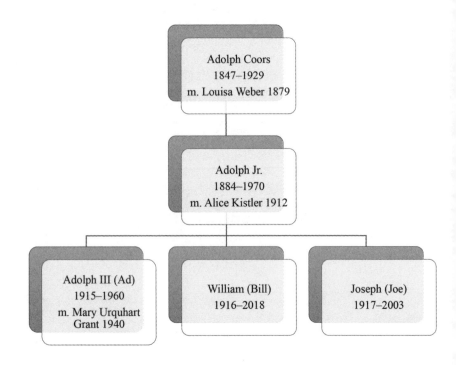

10

Coors

Beer

We don't need marketing. We know we make the best beer in the world.
—WILLIAM COORS

THE NAME COORS CONJURES VISIONS OF BEER BOTTLES AND CLEAR Rocky Mountain spring water. However, this family dynasty from Colorado has also had an indelible impact on American politics since the early 1960s.

ADOLPH COORS
(1847–1929)

The patriarch of the Coors family was born in Prussia in 1847. Adolph Coors was orphaned at fifteen, just as he was starting a three-year apprenticeship with a brewer in Dortmund. He got a job as a bookkeeper to pay for his apprenticeship. Coors worked at several breweries in Germany until he immigrated to the United States when he was twenty-one, arriving in this country as a stowaway on a ship bound for Baltimore. At some point, he changed his name from Kohrs to Coors. He made his way to Chicago, where, after working as a laborer, he found work as a foreman in a brewery. In 1872, at the age of twenty-five, Coors moved to Denver, Colorado, where he would remain for the rest of his life.

An excellent manager of his money, Coors was soon able to buy a bottling firm. Teaming up with Denver confectioner Jacob Schueler, Coors and Schueler bought the abandoned Golden City Tannery in Golden, Colorado, a small town just a dozen miles from Denver. Coors was particularly interested in this property because Clear Creek, a cold mountain stream, ran through it—the perfect water from which to create the perfect beer. Coors soon bought Schueler out and named his brewery Adolph Coors Golden Brewery. Sixteen years later, he was a millionaire.

Coors lived on very little and put all the money he made back into the business. Within a couple of years, he was able to build a malt house, a steam mill, a bottling plant, and a 1,500-ton icehouse. Adolph believed that to create the perfect beer, he had to control every aspect of the process. His motto was "The more we do ourselves, the higher quality we have." He married Louisa Weber in 1879, and by 1890, the same year Coors became a millionaire, they had six children—three sons and three daughters. The Coors family lived modestly as most of the money was poured back into the company.

Because of the distance from Denver and suppliers of malt and bottles, Coors decided to build—and thereby control—his beer empire, from growing his own barley to setting up his own bottling plant. Through absolute control and vertical integration of the Adolph Coors Brewery, Coors was able to create the product he wanted to sell. In 1893 his beer was the only one west of the Missouri to win a medal at the Chicago World's Fair. Coors paid his workers well at sixteen dollars per week and, in return, he wanted a smoothly operating brewery. Every hour, he gave the workers a five-minute break during which "beer boys" ran around the factory floor filling the workers' mugs with free lager.

By the time Coors opened his brewery in Colorado, another German immigrant, Adolphus Busch was already doing very well in the beer business. Located in St. Louis, Missouri, Busch was more interested in quantity than quality and was determined to have the first national brewery. Beer had a very short shelf life—heat and light made the beverage spoil—putting limits on how far the product could be shipped. Busch became the first brewer to pasteurize beer by dipping the bottles into a hot-water bath. This killed the bad bacteria and allowed Busch to ship his beer across the country. Coors believed that subjecting his beer to heat would ruin it, so he refused to pasteurize his product, severely limiting distribution. As historian Dan Baum writes in *Citizen Coors*, "To a craftsman like Adolph Coors, drinking a Missouri beer in Colorado was like steeping a cup of tea in St. Louis to drink in Denver."

In the late nineteenth century, there was a push to ban alcohol. The Women's Christian Temperance Union and Carrie Nation's Anti-Saloon League were organizing in Colorado to "drive Satanic liquor traffic down to its native hell." Colorado women could vote in the state in 1893 and agitated against alcohol. Coors was furious that beer was put in the same category as liquor and argued that beer was itself a temperance drink because it was so much milder than whiskey. Coors could see the temperance movement gathering strength, so he began to diversify his business. The business he picked up would have a dramatic impact on the Coors family bottom line into the twenty-first century. The business was porcelain making, using the abundant clay available around Golden, Colorado.

Until the outbreak of World War I, laboratories in the United States bought chemical porcelain from Germany. Chemical porcelain has to withstand the caustic properties of different chemicals and high fluctuations in temperature. When the German supply was cut off, the call went out for American potteries to start making chemical porcelain. Coors directed his son Adolph Jr. to head up the porcelain division. Adolph Jr. was the perfect person for the job, having graduated from Cornell University with a degree in chemical engineering and, like his father, he was obsessed with quality. Within a year, Coors was the sole supplier in the United States of chemical porcelain.

Liquor, including beer and wine, became illegal in Colorado on January 1, 1916. The day before the liquor ban, Coors ordered all of the beer in the factory, 561 barrels, dumped into the creek, signaling the end of the beer business for the Adolph Coors Brewery. Adolph Coors could have retired at that point. He was worth $2 million and was seventy years old. His daughters were married, and his sons had all followed him into the business. Instead, Coors converted his brewery into a malted milk factory. The brewers also made a near beer called Mannah. Coors kept his employees on but asked them to take a pay cut to help the company get through Prohibition. Rather than gratitude, which Coors expected, the workers went on strike.

Adolph Jr. advised his father to fire the strikers and hire replacements. Coors did, and thus began the conflict between Coors family management and labor that would last well into the twenty-first century.

In 1923, at the age of seventy-six, Adolph Coors finally signed the business over to Adolph Jr. However, not accustomed to leisure time, the old man continued to go to work every day to walk the factory floor. His wife convinced him to do some traveling to the Bahamas, Key West, and the West Coast, and in April 1929, they checked into the Cavalier Hotel in Virginia Beach. Coors's doctor advised a trip to Virginia to build up his strength after suffering a bout of influenza. He and Louisa had recently celebrated their golden anniversary.

Adolph Coors either fell or jumped from his sixth-floor hotel window on the morning of June 5, 1929. The coroner deemed an investigation unnecessary, and the body was shipped back to Denver by train. The *New York Times* obituary stated that Adolph Coors "died suddenly of heart disease as he was dressing for the day." However, historian Dan Baum writes, "I came to be pretty convinced that it was in fact a suicide."

ADOLPH COORS JR.
(1884–1970)

Tapped by his father to run the family business at the age of thirty-nine, Adolph Jr. was a dour figure on the factory floor. Very tall and thin, he always dressed in an Edwardian suit of the deepest black. His three-button jacket was always fastened, topped by a starched color and black bow tie. He wore black, high-button goat-leather shoes.

In 1912, Adolph Jr. married Alice Kistler, and together they had three sons and one daughter. Adolph Jr., like his father, was a strict and distant figure to his children. After reviewing their weekly misdemeanors that he kept track of in a notebook, Adolph Jr. gave his children spankings every Sunday His oldest son, Adolph III, the presumptive heir, suffered from a debilitating stutter, meaning he would be useless as a spokesperson for the company. Adolph III and his youngest brother, Joseph, attended Cornell University, while middle son Bill went to Princeton.

When Prohibition ended at the end of 1933, Adolph Coors Brewery began making beer again. Adolph Jr. knew that beer was a workingman's beverage and that he couldn't afford to alienate labor, so he invited the Brewery Workers Union to organize at the Coors brewery. The union asked for a thirty-six-hour workweek. He also gave the workers an additional month's pay at Christmas as a bonus.

Everyone who worked in the factory called each other by their first names, except for Adolph Jr.—he was always addressed as "Mr. Coors." While the workforce dressed casually, including Adolph Jr.'s sons, who wore khakis and polo shirts, Mr. Coors wore his suit and high-topped dress shoes every day. There was no mistaking who was in charge. Adolph Jr., who died in 1970 at the age of eighty-six, went into the office every day until a couple of days before his death. This meant that although his sons controlled the company's day-to-day business, they still had to answer to Mr. Coors about every decision.

Adolph III, Bill, and Joe—Mr. Coors's sons—for years sat with their desks almost touching as they came to work for the family business. Adolph III was the heir apparent, even though he would never be the front man because of his stutter. Bill and Joe would assume control over various parts of the business. Then everything changed.

On February 6, 1960, while on his way to work, Adolph Coors III was killed when Joe Corbett tried to kidnap him. Adolph III (known as Ad) lived on a ranch with his wife and four children and drove a dozen miles to the factory every morning. Because of road construction, he had to travel the back way, over country roads that took him through the breathtaking landscape of the Rocky Mountain foothills. As he approached a one-lane wooden bridge, he came upon a car stopped on the bridge with the hood up. A man wearing a hat was standing by his vehicle. Ad parked his truck at the end of the bridge, leaving it running and the radio on, as he got out to see if he could help. Corbett, holding a gun, told him to get his hands up, at which point Ad rushed him. Corbett shot twice, hitting Ad in the shoulder with both bullets. There was a struggle, and Ad's glasses and hat were knocked off, as was Corbett's. Ad ended up wrapped in a blanket in Corbett's trunk, who then drove off. Once he realized Ad was dead and would be no good to him, he dumped the body at an out-of-the-way trash heap he'd found weeks earlier while hunting. Corbett went back to Denver and posted a ransom note anyway, even though he was not going to stay around to see if the Coors family complied with his demand for $500,000.

Ever since Charles Lindbergh's baby was kidnapped for ransom in 1932—a plot that ended in tragedy with the baby's death—wealthy and prominent Americans had a fear of being snatched lodged somewhere in their psyche. In 1934 Denver police uncovered a plan to kidnap Adolph Jr. for $50,000 in ransom. The plan was foiled when one of the ringleaders was arrested for stealing a car, but the idea that a Coors could be kidnapped was planted in the collective family's mind.

Adolph Jr. and his wife Louise were on their annual vacation to Hawaii when they heard the news that their son had been kidnapped. They came home and were met by reporters at the Denver airport, where Adolph Jr. commented: "I am dealing with crooks who have something I want to buy: my son. The price is secondary."

The police combed the area for six months before finding Ad's body. During that time, Corbett led the police, and then the FBI (Corbett ended up on the FBI ten-most-wanted criminals list), on a wild goose chase across the continent. First to New Jersey, then to Toronto and Winnipeg, and finally, seven weeks after Ad's body was discovered, to a boarding house in Vancouver, where Corbett gave up without a fight.

Ad's wife, Mary, spent the months before Ad's body was found in a stupor, first from medication from her doctor, then from drinking. Mary and the children moved from the ranch to a wealthy enclave in Denver. The four children went to school with armed guards. Nothing would ever be the same for them. In a cruel turn, Adolph Coors Jr. cut Mary and his four grandchildren out of his will, severing the descendants of Adolph Coors III from the family fortune.

Adolph Coors Jr. died in 1970 at the age of eighty-six. He worked his last day in the brewery on Monday, and by Thursday, he was dead. Dan Baum, historian, writes, "On Friday, work at the brewery continued a usual. Mr. Coors wanted no pauses, no memorials, no funeral." Mr. Coors's body was cremated, and the ashes were scattered.

BILL COORS (1916–2018) AND
JOE COORS (1918–2003)

Bill Coors and his younger brother Joe ran the Coors empire for decades, first under the watchful eye of their father Adolph Jr.; then, after his death in 1970, they were on their own.

In 1959, Coors revolutionized the entire beverage industry with the creation and development of the aluminum can. It had taken five years and $10 million, and the can wasn't perfect, but Coors was making aluminum beverage cans for a little more than a penny per can. Coors was the first American beverage company to fill aluminum cans. Bill Coors, who was instrumental in the can's development, was named Man of the Year by *Modern Metals* magazine. Coors also offered a penny a can for each aluminum can that was returned. By 1990, Coors was operating the biggest aluminum-can plant in the world—manufacturing four billion cans a year, twenty million a day.

Joe and Bill Coors worked together to take Coors from a brewery with a regional distribution to one with a national reach. This happened after their father died because only then could they entertain the idea of marketing and expanding their product line. The brothers brought in members of the next generation—Joe Coors's sons—to learn the family business.

Peter Coors, a Cornell graduate like his father, then earned an MBA at the University of Denver and worked his way up to become president of the company. What Peter found in the early 1970s was a $350 million industrial corporation that kept its records by hand in ledger books. There were no accountants or lawyers on staff, much less a marketing department. Peter was given a seat on the board of the company, along with his uncles and his older brother Jeffrey. He then argued that they hire a director of market research. His uncles were incredulous. What's to research? People drink beer because they like it, so the better the beer, the more they'll drink. Thus began a decades-long struggle for the Coors family and the company. It was a kind of if-it-ain't-broke-don't-fix-it attitude versus the desire to look ahead and plan for the future.

Adding to these internal family struggles, brewery management developed an adversarial relationship with the labor union that represented the plant's workers. After going on strike for almost two years in the mid-1970s, the union folded, and Coors became a nonunion shop. But Coors problems didn't end. The AFL-CIO organized a boycott of Coors products that lasted for a decade and put a hefty dent in their bottom line. One reason the boycott worked was the politics of Joe and Bill.

In the 1970s, Joe Coors put his money and influence into starting the Heritage Foundation, a conservative think tank in Washington. Within a decade, the foundation had an annual budget of more than $10 million and supported more than one hundred scholars and researchers to promote the conservative movement in America. Joe met Ronald Reagan in Palm Springs, California, in the late 1960s and became a mainstay in the campaign to propel Reagan into the White House. With Reagan's election in 1980, Joe Coors was in the president's inner circle that made recommendations about the makeup of his administration, including promoting James G. Watt, who became secretary of the interior.

Bill Coors was also an ultraconservative, whose speeches incurred the wrath of organized labor, civil rights groups, and minorities. Bill instituted lie-detector tests for his workers, asking questions about sexual orientation and subversive activities, according to his obituary in the *New York Times*. The decade-long boycott eventually brought enough pressure on the company that Coors signed agreements with African American and Hispanic groups to increase minorities in all aspects of the business. Bill was also very health conscious and, beginning in the 1970s, a practitioner of Transcendental Meditation. He built a wellness center on the factory grounds for the free use of employees.

Today the Adolph Coors Brewing Company is now known as Molson Coors, reflecting the 2005 merger of the two breweries. When Bill and Joe began in the family business three-quarters of a century ago, the company was a small regional brewery, distributing beer in twelve Western states and producing 145,000 barrels of beer a year. Today, as Molson Coors, the company distributes worldwide and produces over 45 million barrels of beer annually.

III

FAME

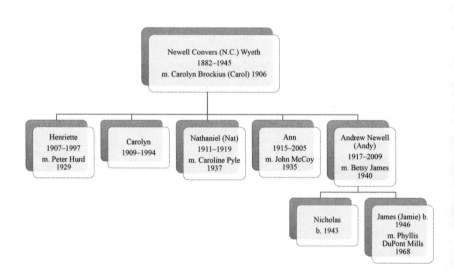

11

Wyeth

Painting Legacy

If you display yourself completely, all your inner soul disappears. You have to keep something to your imagination, to yourself.

—Andrew Wyeth

There may not be a more famous dynasty of painters in America than the Wyeth family. From Newell Convers "N.C." Wyeth, at the turn of the twentieth century, to his son Andrew "Andy" Wyeth (1917–2009), to his son James "Jamie" Wyeth (b. 1946) lies a straight line of influential painters. The second generation—along with Andy—includes his sisters Henriette and Carolyn, both painters, and sister Ann, a composer. But the focus has always been on the three generations of talented Wyeth men who dominated more than a century of American painting.

NEWELL CONVERS "N.C." WYETH
(1882–1945)

Newell Convers "N.C." Wyeth was born to a Swiss American mother, Hattie Zirngeibels and her husband, Newell Wyeth. The family lived in Needham, Massachusetts, on the outskirts of Boston; Hattie's parents lived on the homestead across the road. The Zirngeibel family was very tight-knit. The elder Zirngeibels emigrated from Switzerland in 1855, and Hattie's father got a job working in the greenhouses at Harvard College. He eventually owned several large greenhouses and hybridized many flowers, eventually becoming known as the Pansy Man.

N.C., known as Convers to his family, was a big boy, broad across the shoulders and with some heft to his body. This would become an issue later, as he was frequently admonished by his doctor to lose weight. When he was fully grown, he towered over most men, as he topped six feet. He had the build of a football player but had no interest in sports. He spent his free time with pencil and paper in his hand. A lackluster student, his parents agreed to send him to Mechanic Arts High School in Boston, where he learned drafting. And while N.C. became very skilled at drafting, he never saw himself in this field. He wanted to be a painter. He studied at the Massachusetts Normal Art School, then at the Eric Pape School of Art in Boston, then under the tutelage of George L. Noyes and Charles W. Reed. When three of his friends were accepted to the Howard Pyle School of Art in Wilmington, Delaware (and Chadds Ford, Pennsylvania, in the summers), N.C. knew he had to leave Needham to make the move south. It was 1902.

N.C.'s mother was devastated that he would leave her, and over their lifetimes, they exchanged thousands of lengthy letters where they told each other about the details of their days as well as their innermost thoughts. Hattie's letters revealed her to be a narcissistic, often severely depressed woman. N.C. called it her "homesickness" for her family's life in a small town in the mountains of Switzerland, which she had never experienced firsthand but still yearned for deeply. Although she was born in the States, "prenatal influence asserted itself," wrote N.C. to his friend Sidney M. Chase. "[My grandmother's] longing soul became my mother's inheritance. I can read it in her every letter, in her eyes and her voice." N.C.'s attachment to his mother meant that over the course of his life, he would periodically pack up the family and move back to Needham and his idealized version of home.

At the turn of the twentieth century, Howard Pyle was the most famous illustrator in America. His paintings and ink drawings were found in the most popular magazines of the day, such as *Harper's Weekly* and *Scribner's Monthly*. His career began with black-and-white illustrations and drawings and then moved into color illustrations when it became technically possible to reproduce them in publications. His illustrated children's books, such as *The Merry Adventures of Robin Hood*, vaulted him to prominence. He prided himself on historical accuracy and kept

N.C. Wyeth in the studio with a cowboy model. *Source:* Wikipedia. org/wiki/Andrew_Wyeth.

a collection of costumes and props to be used by models, which N.C. Wyeth would do as well.

Howard Pyle had a Svengali-like influence over his students (who were all men by the time Wyeth joined the brood). Pyle, who was known as the "Master," picked a handful of students carefully. When he looked at students' paintings in the studio at the end of the day, he could leave them trembling from sharp criticism or walking on air from a glowing critique. The pupils joined the Pyles for Sunday dinner, and the favorite students accompanied them on family vacations. The school moved from Wilmington to Chadds Ford during the summer months, where they lived in houses that Washington and Lafayette stayed in during the American Revolution's Battle of the Brandywine. N.C. Wyeth, with his excellent drawing skills and sense of color, soon became Howard Pyle's favorite.

Pyle told his students that they must be artists first and then illustrators. He emphasized drama and emotional content, which, he believed, came from the artist's personal concern with the subject. To this end, many of his students traveled to gain experience with their subjects. For example, Frank Schoonover, the illustrator of Jack London's *White Fang*, visited Hudson Bay to be able to depict the frigid North accurately. Wyeth's first published illustration—of a bucking bronco and rider—appeared on the cover of *The Saturday Evening Post* in 1903. The following year, Joseph Chapin, the art editor at *Scribner's*, sent Wyeth to the American West. N.C. Wyeth, who grew up on depictions of the West by Frederic Remington, traveled to witness and gain experience as a cowboy on a cattle round-up, as a mail carrier by horse between a small town in New Mexico and one in Arizona, and as a visitor to the Navaho reservation. For several years, Wyeth was caught up in Western subjects, as magazines like *Scribner's*, *Harper's*, *McClure's*, and *Outing* regularly sent him commissions for Western stories.

Wyeth complained to Pyle that he didn't give them enough outdoor training. Wyeth yearned to paint the landscape and found the land around Chadds Ford beautiful and compelling. He told his friend Sidney Chase that he believed the students had "missed the great underlying impulses of nature." Wyeth left Pyle in 1906, partly because Wyeth wanted to be a "real painter" and not just an illustrator. For the rest of his life, Wyeth, who was considered one of America's best illustrators during what is called the Golden Age of Illustration, declared that illustration was not his ultimate goal.

After his marriage to Carolyn "Carol" Bockius of Wilmington in 1906, the couple moved to Chadds Ford, where they lived for the rest of their lives. N.C.'s career as an illustrator took off, and he worked for all of the major publications of the day. He also illustrated both children's and adult books and stories, including Robert Louis Stevenson's *Kidnapped* and *Treasure Island, The Last of the Mohicans* by James Fenimore Cooper, *Rip Van Winkle* by Washington Irving, Marjorie Kinnan Rawlings's *The Yearling*, and Mary Johnston's Civil War novels *The Long Roll* and *Cease Firing*. Some of his very best paintings appeared between the covers of these books, characterized by an impeccable sense of drama and narrative storytelling. Wyeth had a way of placing the viewer in the moment of action, whether it was between fighting pirates or with an Indian paddling his canoe through still water. Generations of Americans

An illustration of Beethoven by N.C. Wyeth. *Source:* Library of Congress.

were thrilled by these illustrations, where the colors were always vibrant and the skies dramatic.

Wyeth became wealthy from book illustration, and he and Carol built a house and studio on the edge of the village of Chadds Ford, just up from the old schoolhouse (which they purchased and used as housing for family members). Their land was surrounded by the fields, woods, and rolling hills of the Brandywine River Valley. They had five children: Nathaniel, Henriette, Carolyn, Ann, and Andrew—and N.C. sought to encourage all of their talents. Nathaniel, who became an engineer for DuPont, the only nonartist of the children (Henriette, Carolyn, and Andrew became painters, and Ann was a composer), spent his childhood making precise model ships and miniature furniture.

N.C. Wyeth was a larger-than-life character to his children, like something straight out of one of his illustrations. His hair was dark and curly, and he sported round wire-rimmed glasses. In the studio, N.C. always wore a long painting smock over his shirt and knickers that fell just below the knee. He also wore long socks and high-top sneakers. His paintings were large, sometimes life-sized, and he worked very fast. Later in his career, he painted commissioned murals for buildings, on canvases that would stretch as long as thirty feet.

For N.C., it was all about family—including his parents—or himself. He supervised the painting lessons of Henriette and Carolyn, who both had real talent. He was a hard taskmaster, demanding that they draw solid forms like spheres and cones in charcoal for a year until they had an innate grasp of how to deal with volume. Entranced with Ann's musical abilities, he loved to hear her practicing and composing on the grand piano he bought for her. He also craved the attention he received from his mother through their voluminous exchange of letters.

Andrew, the youngest, was the impish fair-haired child. Born in 1917, he was beset by childhood illnesses and, a debilitating hip problem that kept him at home with tutors. N.C. recognized his unusual artistic ability early on. The boy spent his waking hours drawing or organizing make-believe play sessions with his sisters and some neighborhood kids, where they dressed in costumes collected by N.C. for his illustration work. It wasn't unusual to see a band of kids running through the fields dressed as characters from Robin Hood with Andy playing the lead role.

N.C. spent his entire adult life fretting over what he perceived as the disconnect between illustration and painting. Although, under Howard Pyle's tutelage, he had perfected incorporating drama and storytelling techniques into his illustrations, this was never enough for N.C. His vibrant, luscious illustrations, which had an impact on millions, couldn't match the acclaim he wanted from serious artists. When he stepped outside of illustration, his paintings felt flat and uninspired. When he veered from using his jewel tones, it's as if the life left the paintings. It was rare that a painting of his was accepted into a show, much less won a prize. This feeling of inadequacy would dog him for the rest of his life, particularly once Andrew began showing and selling his work and was taken seriously as an artist.

Like Howard Pyle, N.C. accepted some students whom he then dominated. He often "fixed" their paintings. Two of them went on to marry two of N.C.'s daughters. Peter Hurd hailed from New Mexico, and N.C. loved his very Westerness. He could ride a horse while standing on its back, which impressed all of the Wyeths. Peter charmed the family and ended up marrying the oldest daughter, Henriette. His illustrations, however, looked like Wyeth imitations, and it wasn't until he and Henriette made their way back to New Mexico a decade after marrying that they began to paint in their own style. John McCoy, son of a DuPont executive, also had ambitions as a painter. He graduated from Cornell, studied painting in Paris, and then sought out N.C. to be his tutor. N.C. paired him with Andy in the studio, and John became like a member of the family, taking his meals at the homestead. He and N.C.'s daughter Ann, the composer, married in 1935 and settled a mile from the Wyeth home.

The marriage that would end up being the most problematic for the Wyeth family was that of Nathaniel "Nat" and Caroline Pyle, Howard Pyle's niece. Caroline grew up a couple of miles from the Wyeths—her mother had been a student of Howard Pyle and then went on to marry Pyle's brother. There was competition between the Wyeths and the Pyles, as numerous members of both families painted and showed locally. Howard Pyle, viewed as the founder of the "Brandywine School" of painting, grated on N.C., who spent years trying to shake loose from his connection to the great illustrator. N.C. and Carol viewed Caroline Pyle as "wild" and an inappropriate match for their son. Nat, who was working for DuPont, and Caroline married in January 1937, five months after

Caroline's mother died, making the wedding a somber affair. "It was a depressing day, a depressing ceremony. I could feel it," Andy said later.

In 1920, N.C. bought an old ship captain's house—Eight Bells—in Port Clyde, Maine, which became the family's summer home for years. Every summer, Carol and some subset of kids decamped to the rugged coast of Maine, and N.C. would visit when he was not too tied down with work. In 1925, N.C.'s mother, Hattie, died; N.C. happened to be in Maine, when he heard the news. Bereft, he traveled to Needham, Massachusetts, to sit with his mother's body as it was laid out in the parlor.

In 1943, N.C. Wyeth was sixty-one, and his daughter-in-law Caroline Pyle Wyeth was twenty-nine. Caroline and Nat and their child, Newell, were living in New Jersey, but Nat's war work with DuPont meant he was always away. Caroline, with a small child and again pregnant, was lonely. Trading sugar ration stamps for gas stamps, N.C. began visiting Caroline and his grandson in New Jersey, and when he wasn't there, he began writing Caroline letters. In 1944, after the birth of her second child, he told her that in his eyes, she outshone all the other Wyeth mothers. He had five other grandchildren. "By all accounts, she was a devoted mother, sensitive, merry, bright." But there was more to her than that.

His letters to Caroline were like those of a suitor to his intended. On July 4, 1944, he wrote: "Never before have I felt the craving so intensively to either talk with you, or by letters, to communicate some of the many sharp delineations of feeling that rise and fall these days with such excruciating force. Doubtless you have at times reflected upon the character of some of the letters I have written you and have subtly wondered at some of the personal sentiments expressed in them. Also, those endless and ponderous dissertations on so many topics must give you doubtful pause. Well, it is hardly necessary to remind you that you hold a growing and unique place in my heart and mind. In spirit and person, you have become a shining mark which draws my fire—a very beautiful, resilient, live target."

In January 1945, Nat was transferred by DuPont to the Wilmington plant, and he and Caroline moved into a farmhouse five hundred feet from the Wyeth homestead's front gate. However, Nat was still gone most of the time. Every morning, N.C. stopped by Nat and Caroline's

A powerful image by N.C. Wyeth for U.S. War Bonds during World War II. *Source:* Library of Congress.

house to collect four-year-old Newell in his automobile to take him on the day's errands. That summer, Carol left for Maine, leaving N.C. alone with Caroline and their children.

N.C. encouraged Caroline to write about her moods in poetry and was so entranced by her poems that he copied them and circulated them to the family. No one knows Carol's reaction upon receiving copies of Caroline's poems in the mail, but Carol was depressed and in low spirits that summer and gained back the weight she had lost a couple of years earlier. N.C. introduced Caroline to the great editor Max Perkins of *Scribner's* for his assessment of her poems. Perkins wrote, "Undoubtedly the author has a poetic gift, but as in any other art, it must be disciplined and developed."

There was much discussion in the family about whether N.C. and Caroline had a physical affair as well as an emotional one. Nat recalled walking into the studio one night and finding his father alone with his face smeared with bright red lipstick. It was Caroline's color. N.C. denied anything was going on, but Nat was incredulous and said, "Look, Pa, this has got to stop." Some (including Betsy Wyeth, Andrew's wife) saw it as obsession, whereas Andrew wouldn't rule a physical relationship out, according to biographer David Michaelis.

On October 19, 1945, N.C., as usual, picked up his grandson Newell, and together they drove out into the country to pick up a housekeeper who was going to sweep out Andrew and Betsy's house ahead of their return from Maine. It was a beautiful, warm day, and they stopped along the side of the road to watch a farmer and his wife shucking cornstalks by hand. The woman heard N.C. say to the boy, "Newell, look at this. This is something you must remember because this is something that is passing. You won't see this again. Remember this."

Less than a mile from the Wyeth homestead was a railroad crossing. There was no light or barrier, just a sign exhorting drivers to stop, look, and listen. The crossing was at the top of a small hill, and the trees grew thick on the embankment, making it difficult to see. Inexplicably, N.C.'s car came to a stop on the tracks as a locomotive came bearing down on them. As soon as the engineer saw the car, he slammed on the air brakes and laid on the horn, but the car did not move. He later said that he saw N.C. holding up his arm as if to ward off the train. After hitting the car, the steam engine dragged it 143 feet down the rails before coming to a stop. Newell was thrown from the car and lay dead alongside the tracks, while N.C. was severely crushed by the impact of the collision and had to be cut from the station wagon. A week later, the coroner found that Newell Convers Wyeth had died of a fractured skull and shock. His death was officially ruled an accident.

ANDREW NEWELL WYETH
(1917–2009)

The last child to be born into the large, chaotic artistic family, Andrew Newell "Andy" Wyeth, was the golden child. In photographs of him when he was a boy, Andy, with his curly locks and impish grin, lights up the picture. Doted on by his family, particularly N.C., Andy led a dreamlike childhood filled with free-ranging costumed games like Robin Hood and his gang. Andy always cast himself in the starring role.

Andy was often sick with sinus problems as a young child and had a congenital hip problem that made him walk with his feet splayed. He went to the Chadds Ford elementary school for two weeks of first grade and then convinced his parents to let him stay home. He had a series of tutors for the rest of his education. When N.C.'s student Peter Hurd married Andy's sister Henriette, Peter noticed that twelve-year-old Andy was barely literate. "I didn't know how to read properly," Andy recalled later. "It didn't bother my father. It bothered Pete terribly. I didn't even know my ABCs!"

One thing that N.C. instilled in all of his children was that mood was everything. The facts were secondary. Andy became fascinated by his toy soldiers, which engaged in days-long battles complete with the theatrics of death throes and bombing attacks. "The times I liked best were when I would work out my own little life with my toy soldiers," explained Wyeth. "I built my own stories, and that is the way painting has been to me—a constantly new experience that I want to carry through to the end. They were real little people. I'm not sure I can comprehend the big world. I'm not a big, powerful painter, doing great big forms. That isn't my interest."

By age six, Andy was drawing obsessively. Soldiers, pirates, knights, cowboys, airplanes, cars, trucks, Crusaders, and musketeers made their way into the pages of Andy's sketchpads. Soldiers with guns and bayonets engaged in epic battles filled the pages. By age ten, Andy knew he wanted to be an artist. That was also the year N.C. began to take his son's drawing seriously. He gave him a little watercolor set and showed him how to "let go" and to paint quickly. But in all else, N.C. gave Andy little guidance when he was a boy. He grew up in a sheltered world where his larger-than-life father dominated the landscape. Peter Hurd became Andy's guide to the outside world, taking him on little painting expeditions to the city of Wilmington and helping Andy work on controlling his emotions.

In the studio, Andy was excelling in pen and ink and watercolor. He did some illustrations but found he didn't really like that work. What he liked best was being in Maine and spending the day with his watercolors in an old metal tackle box and a pad of paper and rapidly painting what he saw. He became a master at watercolor, which is not an easy medium. He painted what he saw—a woman gathering driftwood, a man digging clams, a man rowing a dory. "I was sort of flexing my muscles," said Wyeth. "Just soaking up the country. I wasn't ready to express anything. I just let myself go completely. I didn't know any better."

In 1937, at age nineteen, Andrew Wyeth had his first show of watercolors at the Macbeth Gallery in New York City. The Wyeth family traveled from Chadds Ford, while Andy came down from Maine. He was so nervous that he didn't sign his paintings. All twenty-three watercolors sold in two days, and Andy cleared about $500.

Andrew Wyeth primarily painted in two mediums: watercolor, which could provide bursts of color and appealed to the wild and uncontrolled side of Andy's nature, and egg tempera, an old medium used by Renaissance painters like Jan van Eyck. Egg tempera appealed to Wyeth's meticulous side because it allowed him to explore more specificity and detail. Peter Hurd introduced him to egg tempera—showing him how to mix egg yolk with distilled water and then introduce dried pigments. Later,

Andy began using a technique called "drybrush," where he dipped a brush into watercolor, squeezed out most of the color and water, then splayed the bristles with his fingers. The brush left separate, distinct marks on the paper, which could be layered and crosshatched and woven and built upon.

Whether he was painting in Maine or around Chadds Ford, Andy painted people who fascinated him. He placed them in their landscape—a fisherman with his boat, a World War I veteran in his uniform, a woman in her rocking chair. He also painted objects that evoked something bigger, like a table set for breakfast in front of a window (*Groundhog Day*) or a ragged lace curtain blowing in the breeze of an open window (*Wind from the Sea*) or the hook of a man's prosthesis lying on a woodpile (*Field Hand*). These objects became stand-ins for larger subjects.

Wyeth met his future wife, Betsy James, in Maine. Her family had a summer home in Cushing, on the point opposite Eight Bells. Wyeth dropped in to see Betsy's father, an oil painter who had visited N.C.'s studio. Seventeen-year-old Betsy answered the door. It was Andy's twenty-second birthday, and once he met Betsy, he never looked back. On that

The Olson house in Maine. Home of Christina Olson, subject of *Christina's World*. *Source:* needpix.com.

first day, Betsy took him to see Christina Olson—a middle-aged woman who lived with her brother up the road from the James house. Betsy had been visiting Christina and her brother Al since she was ten. She knew that the Olson house was tough for most people to take—it was a beautiful wreck of a place that smelled and was dirty. Andy immediately liked the Olsons. Christina was unable to use her lower limbs and dragged herself everywhere with her strong arms, but Andy saw a proud beauty contained in that body. He spent years depicting different scenes of the Olson place and of Christina, like *Wind from the Sea* and *Weatherside*. Wyeth's most recognizable painting, *Christina's World*, is of Christina Olson dragging herself up a hill toward her house.

Betsy and Andy married a year later, in 1940, and in 1943 had their son Nicholas and three years later their son James "Jamie." In addition to children, they created a partnership in all aspects of Andy's work. He said, "Betsy helped me get rid of all this goddamn French impressionism that I had very strongly in my watercolors." She talked to him about the shock that lay in the lack of color. She pushed him to try for something more, a sense of drama. Over the years, she became responsible for the business end of painting—she named his works, cataloged them, and arranged for them to be framed and sent out. This freed up Andrew to just paint.

After the tragic death of N.C. and Newell in 1946, Andrew painted *Winter 1946*, which depicts a boy running down a hill—a line of fencing and bits of snow trail up the left side of the painting. It's difficult to tell if he's running in control or careening—the earflaps on his hat blowing back from his head give the sense of movement. You can read the emotion in the painting that Andy did while grieving the loss of his larger-than-life father.

Over the years, the prices for Wyeth's watercolors and temperas have skyrocketed—they fetch over a million dollars today. The general public loves and admires Wyeth's work, as seen by the sales of prints of his work and attendance at art shows featuring Andrew Wyeth paintings. The critics, however, have always loved to hate Wyeth. He's been accused of being boring, using a "scatological" palette, and, according to *The New Yorker's*

Peter Schjeldahl, painting "formulaic stuff not very effective even as illustrational 'realism.'"

Andrew Wyeth himself tried to stir up controversy when he revealed fifteen years of paintings that he had kept hidden, even from Betsy. They were primarily nude pictures of Helga, a Chadds Ford woman he met at his neighbors, the Kuerners. She was spending time at the Kuerner farm taking care of old Karl Kuerner. Later, Helga became a companion for Andrew's sister Carolyn, who was living on the homestead, so Andrew could paint her there without creating suspicion. In 1985, when Andy showed Betsy the paintings, there were over 175 watercolor sketches and drawings and 65 finished tempera paintings. He told her he was viewing the Helga paintings as a series. Wyeth's biographer wrote that "Betsy has always dealt with stress by absorbing herself in a project . . . now her project was the exhaustive preparation of the paintings for selling, which Wyeth wanted done immediately." Wyeth never reveled whether he had a physical relationship with Helga.

A year after Betsy saw the paintings, the Wyeths sold almost all of the Helga works to collector Leonard E. B. Andrews. Andrews convinced the National Gallery to exhibit the Helga paintings a year later. Attendance was phenomenal—outpacing a recent Matisse show. The sensationalism surrounding the Helga pictures both vaulted the paintings into the public eye and invited the wrath of art critics. After the exhibition and subsequent tour, Andrews sold the entire collection to a Japanese company.

After what he viewed as the Helga disaster (i.e., the art critics' response, many of whom saw the paintings as much ado about nothing), Wyeth again picked up his brushes and entered a new phase of painting—he began creating pictures that depicted his own life rather than getting at his life obliquely through his paintings of the subjects he loved, like Christina Olson, Karl Kuerner, and Helga. These later paintings, like *Snow Hill*, were about him.

James "Jamie" Wyeth
(b.1946)

Jamie was born to Andrew and Betsy Wyeth three years after his older brother Nicholas. Like his father, Jamie showed an amazing aptitude for drawing early on. He spent six years in public school and then was tutored so he could concentrate on his art. He never studied with his father, as Andrew did with his own father, but was sent up to N.C.'s studio to study under his Aunt Carolyn. She emphasized the fundamentals of drawing. All of her students had to work in charcoal and render geometric shapes until she was satisfied. Not exciting work but essential to a young painter.

Jamie always wanted to paint with oils. He said he became interested in oils because of the way his Aunt Carolyn squeezed it onto her palette. "I could eat it," he said. "Tempera never looked particularly edible. You have to love a medium to work in it. I love the feel and smell of oil." He studied the techniques and compositions of Howard Pyle, who fascinated him. Jamie also produced a large body of work in watercolor.

In 1963, at the age of seventeen, he produced a portrait in oil titled *Shorty*. Shorty was a local Chadds Ford man who worked for the railroad and hadn't talked to anyone but the storekeeper for twenty years. The portrait is exquisite—an unshaven Shorty sitting in a wingback chair. The juxtaposition of the railroad worker with the elegance of the chair is striking.

Jamie moved to New York City in 1965 and for several months studied anatomy at a hospital morgue. He was just nineteen when he produced *Draft Age*—a young man leaning against a wall in wrap-around sunglasses, with curly blond hair slicked back and wearing a well-worn black leather biker jacket. This painting became Wyeth's commentary on the Vietnam War. Wyeth went on to serve in the U.S. Air Force Reserve from 1966 to 1971. During his service, Wyeth took part in an innovative Eyewitness to Space program, sponsored jointly by NASA and Washington's National Gallery of Art. He got to witness and illustrate both launchings and splashdowns. In 1974 Wyeth traveled from Maine to Washington, D.C., to sketch scenes from the Watergate trial in the Senate and Supreme Court.

Wyeth became well-known as a portraitist of famous people, producing likenesses of Lincoln Kirstein, John F. Kennedy, Andrew Wyeth, Rudolf Nureyev, and Andy Warhol. These works are more than just

The Brandywine River Museum in Chadds Ford, Pennsylvania, the foremost repository Wyeth paintings. *Source:* Wikipedia.org/wiki/Jamie_Wyeth.

representations; they reveal the "character" of the individuals. In 1968 he married Phyllis DuPont Mills, a vivacious horsewoman who had been disabled in an automobile accident when she was twenty. She has been one of his painting models for decades (for example *Wolfbane*, 1984; *Night Wind*, 1983; *Whale*, 1978; *And Then into the Deep Gorge*, 1975; and *Excursion Boats, Monhegan*, 1982).

Phyllis and Jamie Wyeth own a farm in the Brandywine River Valley, not far from Chadds Ford, and a house on the island of Monhegan, Maine—a house that was once owned by the artist Rockwell Kent, an artist Jamie greatly admired. Jamie is well-known for his animal portraits, including *Newfoundland* (1971), *Portrait of a Lady* (1968), *Islander* (1975), and *Portrait of a Pig* (1970). *Portrait of a Pig*, a huge painting, seven feet by five, has become one of Wyeth's best-known works.

Some of Wyeth's one-person exhibitions have included those at the Pennsylvania Academy of Fine Arts, Greenville Museum of Art (South Carolina), Portland Museum of Art (Maine), Columbia Museum of Art, Farnsworth Art Museum, Brandywine River Museum, and Museum of Fine Arts (Boston).

Jamie Wyeth's works are included in many public collections, including those of the Terra Museum of American Art, National Gallery of Art, National Portrait Gallery, John F. Kennedy Library, Museum of Modern Art, Joslyn Art Museum, Farnsworth Art Museum, Delaware Art Museum, Brandywine River Museum, Morgan Library and Museum, Museum of Fine Arts, Boston, Whitney Museum of American Art and Bowdoin College Museum of Art.

Phyllis Wyeth, who died in January 2019, was a respected carriage driver and accomplished Thoroughbred breeder and owner. At her racing stable, she bred the famed horse Union Rags, who would become her champion horse and winner of the Belmont Stakes in 2012. Phyllis and Jamie had no children, bringing the Wyeth painting dynasty to an end.

When asked about the three generations of Wyeth artists, Thomas Padon, director of the Brandywine River Museum of Art, summarized: "Just as there's a remarkable continuity in the three generations of Wyeth family artists in the sense of their shared creativity and abiding sense of place, there are interesting differences that set them apart in distinct ways. Taken together, their body of work is one of the major achievements in American art."

James Duff, director emeritus of the Brandywine River Museum of Art, adds, "N.C. Wyeth, Andrew Wyeth, and Jamie Wyeth are being increasingly recognized for their unique contributions to American art, and their importance will continue to grow through the decades with recognition of their amazing technical abilities, their perspectives on the human condition, and the sheer beauty of their accomplishments."

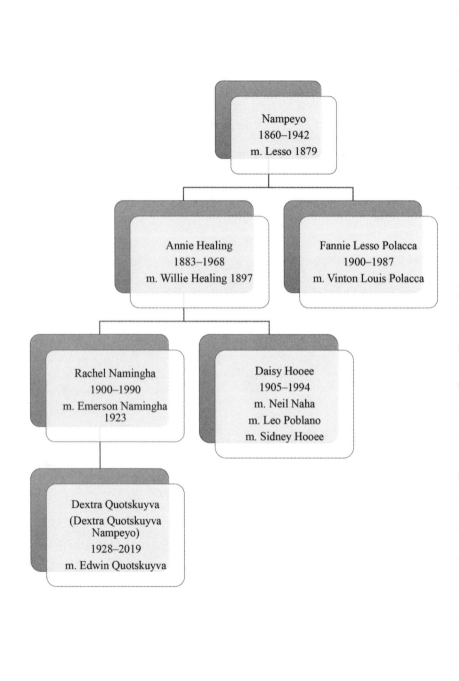

Nampeyo
1860–1942
m. Lesso 1879

Annie Healing
1883–1968
m. Willie Healing 1897

Fannie Lesso Polacca
1900–1987
m. Vinton Louis Polacca

Rachel Namingha
1900–1990
m. Emerson Namingha
1923

Daisy Hooee
1905–1994
m. Neil Naha
m. Leo Poblano
m. Sidney Hooee

Dextra Quotskuyva
(Dextra Quotskuyva
Nampeyo)
1928–2019
m. Edwin Quotskuyva

12

Nampeyo

Hopi-Tewa Potters

"Others were jealous," said one of Nampeyo's grandchildren. "She used to leave her clay outside the house, and one day she knew someone had done something to it. She tasted it, and they had mixed salt in the clay."

NAMPEYO (C.1857–1942), A HOPI-TEWA WOMAN, IS ARGUABLY THE most famous potter of American Indian pottery. Her work, and that of her descendants, put Southwest American Indian pottery on the map and is prized by collectors around the world. Until the twentieth century, their pots were unsigned, as was the Hopi and Tewa custom of not seeking individual recognition. The tiny, unassuming potter, who was doing what she loved to do, was likely unaware of her fame as she lived her long life on the mesa where she was born.

NAMPEYO
(c.1857–1942)
In the northeast quadrant of Arizona, snug against the New Mexico border, is the land of the Hopi Indians. Their land, primarily three mesas and surrounding lowlands, is contained within the much larger Navajo landholdings. There is no love lost between the two tribes, and it's been this way for centuries. The Hopi moved from the lowlands to occupy the mesas in the seventeenth century to better protect themselves from raids by Utes, Navajo, Apaches, and Comanches. The eighteenth-century Hopi leaders asked a group of Tewa Indians, another Pueblo Indian group from New Mexico, to relocate to the Hopi mesas to help them defend themselves from marauding neighbors. The Tewa came because the Hopi

promised them land. The Hopis then reneged on their offer. This moment sowed the seeds of mistrust between the two tribes. Despite this, when the Utes raided the area, the Tewa fought back. The Hopi leaders then gave the Tewa land on top of First Mesa for their own village, but trust between the two tribes never recovered.

Tewas call their village Tewa Village, but it is commonly known as Hano. Each Tewa clan built stone dwellings—pueblos—as did the Hopi. Because it was a matriarchal society, when a daughter married, the son-in-law moved into his wife's home. Rooms were added above the original house as the clan increased. Kivas, underground chambers, played an important role in the social and ceremonial life of each Tewa clan, and it's where ceremonies, dances, clan functions, and social gatherings of the men took place.

Nampeyo was born into the Corn Clan around 1857. No one knows the precise year because time was not calculated that way by the Tewa, who lived by the natural dictates of the seasons. Nampeyo's father, Quootsva, came from the Hopi Snake Clan and lived in Walpi until his marriage to White Corn. Nampeyo, whose name means "snake that does not bite" in Tewa, was White Corn's only daughter. She had three older brothers, Palaccaca (who later adopted the name Tom Polacca), Kano, and Patuntupi (later known as Squash).

White Corn, like many Hopi and Tewa women, made utilitarian clay pots. She taught Nampeyo where to dig for the clay, how to wash the impurities from it, and how to fire the pots. They made cooking pots and storage jars, and bowls of all sizes. When men worked in the cornfields, they carried small pottery canteens. The potters also made larger canteens that could hold three to six gallons of water that the women would take down to the stream below the mesa. They secured the canteen on their backs with shawls tied around their foreheads that held the jug in place. When full, the women had to lean forward to balance the heavy load on their backs while climbing the steep mesa trail, leaving many of the older women permanently bent from the arduous daily chore.

The Hopi were called Moqui or Moki by the United States government, which created a Moqui Pueblo Agency in 1869, but the federal government did not acknowledge or protect Hopi lands until 1882. Prior to 1882, more and more land was ceded to the Navajo until the mesa peoples were surrounded. The Hopi culture seemed impenetrable to the white agents sent by Washington to establish authority over the people of the mesa. Many recommended that they be moved from their homes and reestablished in government-built houses to be "Americanized." Fortunately, that didn't happen.

Tom Polacca, Nampeyo's older brother, became a respected Tewa leader. He learned English—likely from a Mormon missionary who also converted Polacca. Tom struck up a friendship with Thomas Keam, who opened the first trading post in the area. The Hopi and Navajo came in droves and bartered hides, sheepskins, blankets, rugs, baskets, and pottery for flour, sugar, coffee, dry goods, calico, pots and pans, and cast-iron frying pans.

During the late 1870s and 1880s, museums and universities developed an insatiable desire for American Indian artifacts. John Wesley Powell, the first director of the Smithsonian's Bureau of Ethnology, believed the bureau's most important task was to research and compile information about native peoples. He focused on the Southwest, where he believed ancient cultures remained relatively unchanged by outsiders. Shockingly, Powell and Spencer F. Baird, secretary of the Smithsonian (Powell's boss), "reasoned that native people were soon to become extinct, so an immediate collection of artifacts should be made for future anthropological study." Over the next decade, literally tons of artifacts, including clothing, baskets, kachina dolls, toys, religious objects, blankets, looms, cradleboards, gourds, dance masks, stone implements, and pottery, were taken or bought from village households. Artifacts were also taken from sites excavated in both the Zuni and Hopi regions.

In 1879, Nampeyo married Lesso, of the Horn Clan from Walpi, and together they would have five children: Annie (1883), William Lesso (1893), Nellie (1896), Wesley (1899), and Fannie (1900). Nampeyo and Lesso lived just above Sikyatik, an ancient site that was excavated on the side of First Mesa. The artifact collectors had a hard time getting their horses and wagons up the narrow path to First Mesa so they blasted out a road and in the process destroyed one of the kivas. Concurrently, the Atlantic and Pacific Railroad laid tracks across northern Arizona, making the Hopi mesas more accessible. The Hopis went from being completely cut off from the modern world to becoming the object of study and curiosity by ethnologists, painters, writers, photographers, visitors, and missionaries. In 1882, President Chester A. Arthur signed an executive order defining the boundaries of the "Moqui Reserve." No one consulted the Hopi, and to this day there are still conflicts with the Navajo over land claims. Throughout the 1880s, collectors gathered Hopi objects with abandon, including ancient pots and potsherds from ruins and burial sites. The impact of this collecting brought changes in the Hopi way of life. Hopi were encouraged by outsiders to give up ancestral vessels and commonplace objects, and it soon became apparent to them that if the white men were willing to trade more goods for ancestral pots, why not make more pots? In the 1890 census, 365 Hopi women on the mesas stated their occupation as "Potter." By 1900, as the collecting frenzy lagged, that number was down to two—Nampeyo and one other.

Hopi-Tewa potter Nampeyo decorating a pot. *Source:* Library of Congress.

One consequence of the increasing number of visitors was the transmission of diseases. Epidemics of smallpox, influenza, tuberculosis, dysentery, and trachoma (a highly contagious, chronic conjunctivitis) ripped throughout the mesas, exacerbated by crowded and unsanitary living conditions. Dr. Joshua Miller became an avid collector of native artifacts during the 1880s. Concerned about the welfare of the Hopi people, he voluntarily ministered to them during the summer months, often accepting native objects for payment. At some point in the 1890s, he treated Nampeyo's eyes for trachoma; in return she gave him a large canteen painted with a kachina design. Trachoma alternately goes into remission and then recurs to produce granulation, scarring, and eventual opacity of the cornea. If untreated with antibiotics, it can produce blindness in about twenty years. Periodically, Nampeyo was treated with an antiseptic solution, which checked the disease for a time but did not cure it. Her trachoma would eventually render her almost blind and unable to paint her own pots.

Nampeyo had emerged as the foremost potter among the Hopi. She was often photographed sitting on a blanket outside her house with her pots for sale displayed around her. She was enormously prolific around the turn of the twentieth century, producing exquisitely crafted and painted pots and bowls based on the designs she saw on ancient pots. According to scholar Barbara Kramer, "By 1900, Nampeyo created a personal, contemporary style known only as 'Hopi Revival' pottery during her lifetime. She was prolific and she had an artist's eye of balance. She had a sense of whimsy and she continually improved."

Great care went into Nampeyo's pottery. First she dug her clay from several sources and let it dry. Then she placed the dry clay on a large rock and pulverized it. The pulverized clay was put into a container of water and mixed into a wet paste. Then, as one of her grandchildren explained: "She put her feet in there to get out all the pebbles. They squeeze out between her toes and she throws them away." The cleaned paste was transferred to a flat stone where Nampeyo kneaded it with her hands until it was a smooth consistency, removing any additional foreign substances that might cause a pot to break during the firing process. "You have to pound it like that with your hand to break all the bubbles out, and you have to

Nampeyo surrounded by her pots. *Source:* Library of Congress.

work it with your hand again and pound it until it all sticks together solid," explained Nampeyo's grandchild. Finally, Nampeyo would rub two pieces of fine sandstone together to create fine sand, which she added to the clay to make it harder and less likely to break. If the clay was too dry, she added water. If it was too wet, she set it in the sun to dry.

When she was ready to work on a pot, Nampeyo would break off a small piece of prepared clay and work it with her thumbs to create a bottom for a pot, which she then placed in a dish or pan for stability. She'd break off more pieces of clay and rolled each between her palms to make a long coil. The pot was built up one coil at a time, Nampeyo pressing and smoothing each to the coil below it. She worked quickly and with wet hands to avoid having the clay dry out. As she built the pot, she used the rind of a gourd or squash to smooth the pot both inside and out. If the pot got to the point where she felt the shape wouldn't support more wet clay, Nampeyo let the half-built pot dry until more coils could be added. This step might be repeated several times until she got the shape and size she desired. Finally, the last coil would be added and the opening shaped, and the pot would be set aside to dry thoroughly.

The dry pot was then rubbed with a smoother made of fine sandstone that left a slightly gouged, grainy surface. After this, she'd apply a thin slip (liquid clay) of white clay to the surface with a swab of wool, and the pot was again set aside to dry. Final polishing was done with a smooth stone that was continually dipped into water.

Nampeyo used natural materials she gathered from the land for her paints. Red, white, and brown paints were all made from minerals that were ground on a slab and mixed with water. The black paint was made from beeweed or mustard plant that was boiled down to a thick syrup and then dried on a slab or cornhusk. Once dried, a small piece was dissolved in just enough water to achieve the desired color and consistency.

Her brushes were made from yucca leaves chewed at the end to allow the fibers to separate. She worked rapidly to cover the vessels with spontaneous designs—fine lines, geometric patterns, broad sweeping scrolls. When she was satisfied, the pot was once more set aside to dry.

When she was ready for firing, Nampeyo created her "kiln." A layer of dried sheep dung, or sometimes soft coal, was laid within a circular ridge of sand. Then it was lit. The dried pots were set nearby to warm. Several rocks or a grate were placed on top of the smoldering dung to hold the unfired pots. The pots were carefully covered with fragments of broken pottery to shield them from the flames. Slabs of dried dung were laid over top of the pots to form a dome. This dung gradually ignited from the smoldering base and was allowed to burn out over several hours.

After this entire process, a pot could come out of the firing with cracks or bubbles, or it could break. Making pottery was never far from disappointment.

At the turn of the twentieth century, when Nampeyo was about forty, photographs and reports about the potter often included or mentioned her daughter Annie, who was about twenty-five at the time. Annie learned from Nampeyo and inherited her quiet temperament. The two often worked together, making pottery to sell. The mother-daughter team was fast and could produce a volume and diversity of fine pots, making them the envy of other potters on the mesa. "Others were jealous," said

Nampeyo building a kiln to fire her pottery. *Source:* Library of Congress.

one of her grandchildren. "She used to leave her clay outside the house, and one day she knew someone had done something to it. She tasted it, and they had mixed salt in the clay."

Photographer Edward S. Curtis, known for his photographs of native peoples and the disappearing Western landscape, took photographs of Nampeyo when he visited the mesa many times between 1900 and 1919. His beautiful images show Nampeyo at work and sitting with her pots. Adam Clark Vroman, another photographer, accompanied an archaeological team to the mesa in time to witness and document the Snake Dance. Vroman took several photographs of Nampeyo and Annie, and in one photograph, he shows four generations of Corn Clan women: White Corn (Nampeyo's mother), Nampeyo, Annie, and Annie's daughter Rachel. Knowing there would be many visitors to witness the biannual Snake Dance ceremony (a two-day ritual that ends with a naked priest placing rattlesnakes in his mouth before setting them free), Nampeyo and Annie had dozens of beautiful vessels available for sale. The Snake Dance ceremony was closed to non-Native outsiders in the late 1980s.

Juan Lorenzo Hubble Sr. bought Thomas Keam's trading post, which sat at the base of First Mesa. Lorenzo Sr. had a long career as a Navajo trader and art collector. Shortly after purchasing Keams Canyon, he compiled a catalog that described "Navajo Blankets & Indian Curios" and "Nanpea pottery; the only pottery that compares with the old in color, finish and design."

Lorenzo Sr. began a mutually beneficial relationship with the Fred Harvey Company. Fred Harvey, an Englishman, created a company to manage hotels and restaurants developed along the Atchison Topeka & Santa Fe Railway lines. The company established the Indian Department within the Harvey hotels. The Indian Department collected curios and the finest native crafts to be shown in exhibits and sold in the hotels. The Harvey Company identified Nampeyo's pieces, which could command a higher price, with stickers that read "Made by Nampeyo, Hopi."

In 1901, the railway completed a spur line from Williams, Arizona, to the rim of the Grand Canyon. They built a chalet-style eighty-room hotel named El Tovar, where they provided luxury with a view. In their art gallery, they sold work by known artists who painted at the canyon. The Harvey Company asked Mary Colter to design a building to be built next to the hotel where guests could purchase curios and watch Indian craftsmen demonstrate their skills in weaving, basketry, pottery, and jewelry making. Colter designed the three-story Hopi House that was then constructed entirely by Hopi workmen. The Harvey Company sought Hopi craftsmen to come to the canyon and work in the Hopi House. They would be given free travel and room and board while they were there.

Nampeyo and her family volunteered to be in residence when the Hopi House opened at the beginning of 1905. The group consisted of four men, two women, and five children: Nampeyo, Lesso, Annie and her husband, Willie, and two adult sons of Nampeyo and Lesso. The young children were Annie's and Nampeyo's. They were advertised this way: "These quaintly-garbed Indians on the housetop hail from Tewa, the home of Nampeyo, the foremost noted pottery-maker in all Hopi-land. Perhaps you will be so fortunate as to see Nampeyo herself . . . Go inside and see how these gentle folk live. The rooms are little and low, like their small statured occupants. The Hopis are making 'piki,' twining the raven black hair of the 'mamas' in big side whorls, smoking corncob pipes, building sacred altars, mending moccasins—doing a hundred un-American things. They are the most primitive Indians in America, with ceremonies several centuries old."

Nampeyo and Annie would only work with their own clay, which had to be sent for when the clay in the two small boxes they brought with them was gone. Nampeyo and her family stayed in Hopi House for three months and wanted to get home by April 1 to plant their corn. When the second group of Hopi arrived, the two potters in the group felt ashamed of their own skills when they saw Nampeyo's work. They produced pots that didn't hold a candle to the work of their predecessor.

In 1910 Nampeyo and her family made one more trip off the mesa to attend the second United States Land and Irrigation Exposition being held in the Chicago Coliseum. A brown stucco mission building was built in the coliseum where the Hopi would live for the duration of the exposition. They traveled fifteen hundred miles, bringing everything they needed with them, first by wagon and then by rail. All travel and living expenses were paid. The newspaper wrote: "Nampeyo, squaw, regarded as the greatest maker of Indian pottery alive. She is frequently consulted by the eminent scientists of the country with reference to what she knows about pottery making. Lesso, a famous Indian dancer, is with the party." That was the last time Nampeyo ever left the mesa.

Within twenty years, Nampeyo had gone from displaying and selling her magnificent pots from a rug placed in front of her house to gaining a much wider audience. As people became familiar with her work through photographs and her visits to the Grand Canyon and Chicago, she could easily sell every pot she made. Her pottery was being purchased by Lorenzo Jr. and Lorenzo Sr. for resale at their trading posts and by representatives of the Fred Harvey Company.

Nampeyo produced pottery from 1876 until 1939, and for almost forty of those years her eyesight was failing. She then entered into a kind of cooperative production of her pottery as one of her daughters or granddaughters worked alongside her.

Much has been made of Nampeyo's gorgeous and artistically rendered designs. There's much speculation as to how Nampeyo became inspired to make pottery based on prehistoric designs. Researchers sometimes refer to her style as Sikyatik Revival after the protohistoric site by that name on First Mesa. It might also have been market driven, as it's likely that trader Thomas Keam, who opened a trading post at First Mesa in 1875, encouraged Nampeyo and other potters to supply work for the growing tourist market. Knowing how well ancient wares sold, Keam suggested that they be used as models. Both Lesso and Nampeyo visited Sikyatki when it was being explored by archaeologists and copied designs they saw on potsherds. Perhaps Nampeyo found these design elements meaningful in addition to being beautiful.

As her eyesight diminished, Nampeyo produced pots that included some tactile work. Nampeyo continued to shape vessels that others painted for her. She didn't need her eyesight to create her pots as her hands remembered how to do the work. Nampeyo returned to making the large-diameter, flat-shouldered jars she had made at the turn of the century.

ANNIE HEALING (1883–1968) AND
FANNIE LESSO POLACCA (1900–1987)

Annie Healing (1883–1968) was the first child born to Nampeyo and Lesso, and she learned, as a young girl, how to create clay vessels by watching her mother work. Soon she was creating her own pots, and by the time she was twenty, she was a skilled potter. There are several photographs taken just after the turn of the twentieth century that show Annie as a young woman sitting with Nampeyo in front of their house with pots displayed on a rug. At that point, Annie worked with red clay slip, so the red-colored bowls can be identified as hers. Although her painted lines were not as fine as Nampeyo's, she exhibited a strong design sense, adapting some of Nampeyo's designs to make them her own. The lines blurred between Nampeyo's work and Annie's since so few of the pots were signed, particularly before the 1930s. And it's likely that many of the pots were cooperatively produced after Nampeyo began to lose her sight. Annie, too, suffered from ill health—her eyesight was also poor, and she had arthritis that was exacerbated by making pots. There are only a few known pots bearing her name.

Fannie Lesso Polacca, (1900–1967). Fannie was Annie's sister and is best known for perpetuating the work of her mother. By the early 1920s, she was also working with Nampeyo.

NAMPEYO'S GRANDDAUGHTERS

Rachel Healing Namingha (1900–1990), Annie's oldest daughter, was the same age as her Aunt Fannie and likely worked alongside her mother, aunt, and grandmother making pots. She was considered a traditional potter, and her decorative work was classic. She did not approve of innovations, according to authors Mary Ellen and Laurence Blair. Rachel and her husband, Emerson Namingha, had seven children, and among their descendants, there are many potters, artists, and carvers.

Daisy Hooee Nampeyo (1905–1994) was Annie's daughter and Rachel's younger sister. Like her sister, Rachel, Daisy learned pottery from her mother, her Aunt Fannie, and her grandmother. However, Daisy's artistic trajectory veered sharply away from the other Nampeyos. At age ten, she attended the Indian boarding school in Phoenix with her older brothers but was sent home after it became clear her vision was failing. She had the same viral condition that her grandmother had—trachoma.

Ceramic pot created by Dextra Quotskuwa Nampeyo. *Source:* photo by Carol Highsmith, Library of Congress.

Daisy's eyes got so bad that she developed cataracts and had to stay in a dark room.

Anita Baldwin, a wealthy heiress from California, was visiting the area to learn about Hopi music when she heard about Daisy. She went to see the girl and told her parents that she would like to take Daisy to California to have her cataracts removed to restore her sight. Daisy left First Mesa and for the next decade lived with Anita Baldwin during the school year and visited her family on First Mesa during the summers. Baldwin recognized Daisy's talent for art, and when she finished high school, Baldwin sent her to study art at L'Ecole des Beaux Arts in Paris, where Daisy excelled in sculpture. When she finished her studies, Anita joined Daisy for an around-the-world trip to see art from different cultures.

When she was twenty-three, Daisy came home to Arizona for good. Through marriage, she ended up living in the Zuni pueblo community. During the rest of her life, she did sculpture, pottery, and silversmithing (she married a silversmith). Like her sister, Rachel, her reputation grew, and her pots and bowls were sought by collectors, who went to Zuni to buy directly from the artist.

Dextra Namingha Quotskuyva, also known as Dextra Quotskuyva Nampeyo (1928–2019), is probably the best known of Nampeyo's descendants. Daughter of Rachel, Dextra didn't take a keen interest in pottery until 1967, but then she jumped in with both feet. Like her great-grandmother, she searched nearby ruins for pottery shards for design inspiration. She used traditional designs until her mother died in 1990; then she branched out. She eschewed using a kiln and experimented with ancient firing techniques outdoors—much like Nampeyo once did—using soft coal, corncobs, and sheep dung. Her paints were made from minerals and vegetables. As a teacher, Dextra was invaluable in keeping the traditional Hopi pottery tradition alive. Dextra participated in major museum and gallery exhibitions across the United States and received numerous honors, including being designated an Arizona Living Treasure in 1995 and receiving a Lifetime Achievement Award from the Arizona State Museum in Tucson 1998.

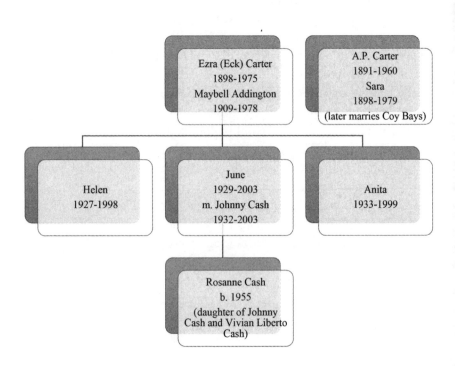

Ezra (Eck) Carter
1898-1975
Maybell Addington
1909-1978

A.P. Carter
1891-1960
Sara
1898-1979
(later marries Coy Bays)

Helen
1927-1998

June
1929-2003
m. Johnny Cash
1932-2003

Anita
1933-1999

Rosanne Cash
b. 1955
(daughter of Johnny
Cash and Vivian Liberto
Cash)

13

Carter Family

Music of the People

My father always said that what amazed him was that they were good, but they didn't seem to know how good *they were.*
—SON OF RECORD PRODUCER RALPH PEER

THE MUSICIANS IN THE CARTER AND CASH FAMILIES ARE WELL-KNOWN to anyone interested in country and Appalachian folk music. The Carter Family and then the Carter Sisters and Mother Maybelle managed to make money during the Depression and bring music to the lives of millions through the radio. When June Carter married Johnny Cash, she brought a semblance of balance to the hard-partying Cash. Their combined families could be considered the First Family of country and folk music for almost a century.

MAYBELLE ADDINGTON CARTER
(1909–1978)
Maybelle Addington Carter was the doyenne of country and Appalachian folk music throughout the first half of the twentieth century. Born in 1909 in tiny Nicklesville, Virginia, almost snug up against the Tennessee border, Maybelle Addington grew up in a large musical family. Her talents became apparent when she quickly learned how to play her mother's autoharp as a child. She then moved on to "banjo pickin'," winning first prize in a Copper Creek banjo contest when she was only twelve. Her older brothers bought a guitar when Maybelle was thirteen, and she developed a unique style of playing the instrument. Her playing style was described by historian and musician Mike Seeger as "a fluid, flowing,

A.P., Sara, and Maybelle Carter as the popular Carter Family. *Source:* Wikipedia.org/wiki/Carter_Family.

rhythmic sound, a way of playing the melody that was plain enough so that you could understand what it was, yet still brought you in because it had rhythm and life to it." This distinctive style of playing would become known as the "Carter scratch."

Many of the songs played by the Addingtons had been passed down through generations of the family—old-timey songs like "Weeping Willow Tree" and "Sugar Hill" and "I Ain't Gonna Work Tomorrow." The Addingtons couldn't read music, so they learned the tunes and played by ear. Maybelle also loved church music. She went to Methodist Holiness revivals just to hear those hymns, which one author described as having the "rhythmic, free-form crackle of old slave spirituals."

The Addingtons lived on one side of Clinch Mountain, and the Carters lived on the other. The Addington side was called Rich Valley, and the Carter side was called Poor Valley. Sara Dougherty, Maybelle's cousin, married Alvin Pleasant "A. P." Carter when Maybelle was six. Maybelle ended up marrying A. P.'s brother Ezra (known as Eck) when she was seventeen and moved to Maces Spring, Carter's hometown, up and over Clinch Mountain. Maybelle and Sara, now sisters-in-law, became very close. Sara had a distinctive deep voice and played the autoharp, and she and Maybelle played and sang together.

A.P. was a fiddler with a quavering bass voice. He was a restless fellow. He couldn't sit still for long and spent hours walking the railroad tracks that ran through Poor Valley. But he was a great fiddler, and he knew his music, and when he heard Sara and Maybelle singing together, he also knew they were good—very good. In 1927 A.P., Sara, and Maybelle headed to Bristol—twenty-five very long miles away on curving dirt roads—to record songs for Ralph Peer of the Victor Company. Peer told A.P. he would pay them fifty dollars for every song he recorded, which to the Carters was a fortune.

Ralph Peer had an arrangement with the Victor Company that he would take no salary but would get royalties for every record sold and would hold the copyrights to all the songs he found. The Victor Company was anxious to get into the growing hillbilly music field because, as they rightly determined, it could be a potential goldmine. Peer needed musicians who could write their own songs or finesse the traditional songs so he could copyright them. When the Carters showed up in the sweltering, stuffy warehouse where Peer was recording, he wasn't expecting much. But when they began to play and sing, Peer was astounded. Sara was the lead voice on the four songs they recorded that night, with A.P. playing fiddle and Maybelle on guitar. They recorded two more songs the following morning and left town $300 richer. Years later, Ralph Peer's son said, "My father always said that what amazed him was that they were good but they didn't seem to know *how good* they were."

Two 78 rpm records of the Carters were released that year, and both sold well, particularly in the South. Peer asked them to come to New Jersey the following spring to record at Victor's studio. The Carter's— now called The Carter Family—prepared twelve original songs, some written by them, others rounded up from neighbors and friends. They also reworked church songs as well and took them all to the New Jersey studio for their two-day recording session. They had to make sure each song was no more than three minutes long (the side of a record). The

Carters left New Jersey with $600 in their pockets, an amount equal to a year's pay.

Those twelve songs turned into twelve hits for the Carter Family. Sara's lone, haunting voice spoke to all kinds of audiences, as did their tight, small-group harmonies. Maybelle's guitar playing—her Carter Scratch—became the most widely imitated guitar style in music. She provided the rhythmic beat as well as smooth melody lines. Her Hawaiian-style-slide-guitar playing was like that favored by the Black blues musicians around the South. As a way to promote their records, A.P. convinced Sara and Maybelle to go on the road giving "entertainments," or concerts, in towns that had record stores. They'd perform in schools or churches, or any place that was big enough to hold a crowd.

The Carter Family records were flying off the shelves, so Peer asked them back to New Jersey to record more songs. A.P. again scoured the countryside for original songs and those they could adapt, so that Peer could hold the copyright. By now, Peer was acting as their manager. A.P. would assign the copyrights to Peer, who would then dole out the royalties, of course keeping behind the lion's share of the take. The Carters were bringing in hundreds of dollars each month. For the first time, the Carters had money. A.P. and Eck bought more land, and Sara bought new dresses and hats and a fur stole. Maybelle bought clothes and china. By the end of 1930, the Carter Family had sold seven hundred thousand records.

In the early 1930s, the Bays family, cousins of the Carters, moved to Maces Springs because they wanted to be near family. Three of the children were sick with tuberculosis, and, one by one, they died. One of the Bays cousins—Coy Bays—came to visit, and he and Sara Carter fell in love. Sara had three children, was married to A.P., and was one-third of the Carter Family musical group. It finally got to the point where the Bays family knew they had to move because of the affair. They sold everything they could, loaded up the car, and headed out of Poor Valley on their way to New Mexico. Sara left A.P. and the kids and went back over the mountain to Rich Valley to live in her aunt and uncle's house—the people who raised her after her mother died. A.P. took the kids back and forth over the mountain to stay with Sara and would then go off in search of more songs.

Not only did Sara's leaving break up the nuclear family, it also threatened to break up the musical family. Ralph Peers set another recording date in June 1933, and Sara at first wanted nothing to do with it but soon realized this was her only chance to earn money. She headed back over the mountain and moved in with Maybelle and Eck so that she, Maybelle, and A.P. could work on some new songs. They recorded sixteen songs in New Jersey, but only half of them were released. It was the heart of the Great Depression, and record sales had slumped, so the music money was drying up. Peers left RCA Victor and took the Carters with him to a new conglomerate called American Recording Company (ARC). The first recording date was May 1935, and the Carter Family recorded forty songs over four days, a record for them. They were now getting seventy-five dollars per song, so A.P., Sara, and Maybelle walked away with $1,000 each. ARC wanted to get a cut on their old hits so the Carter Family recorded new versions of "Keep on the Sunny Side," "River of Jordan," "Single Girl, Married Girl," "Wildwood Flower," "My Clinch Mountain Home," "Little Darlin's Pal of Mine," and "I'm Thinking Tonight of My Blue Eyes." They also rerecorded "Will the Circle Be Unbroken," which had never been released by RCA.

It had been three years since Sara had seen Coy Bays, and it was clear that her marriage was over, so she met with a lawyer and filed for divorce. A.P. was granted custody of the children. Fortunately, this did not dissolve the musical partnership. During 1936 and 1937, the Carters cut almost sixty songs for their new label, Decca. Ralph Peer was relieved.

Maybelle was the most adventuresome musician of the three. She could play a tune after hearing it once, and on any stringed instrument she picked up. Eck, her husband, was the one who understood that with Maybelle's musical abilities, there was a bright future ahead of them. Eck had a good steady job on the mail train, which he loved, but he also understood that the music business could bring real wealth. He bought Maybelle a Gibson L-5 archtop in 1929 for $275—an enormous sum of money at that time—but he knew it was a good investment.

The radio job came out of nowhere. Consolidated Royal Chemical Corporation would buy time on XERA—the biggest radio station of them all—outside of Del Rio, Texas, if the Carter Family would do two shows a day for six months. They'd get $75 a week per person with six months of paid vacation. That's about $4,000 per year each. Who could say no to that? Maybelle, Eck, A.P., Sara, and Maybelle's youngest, five-year-old Anita, piled into the car and headed south. XERA transmitted from a little concrete building in Mexico just over the Rio Grande River. The radio station had such a powerful transmitter that it reached into the homes of people across the United States and into Canada. The Carters put together a show of music, and announcers did the hard sell of the products. One night, Sara dedicated a song to Coy Bays, whom she had not heard from in six years. He listened to the song over the radio in California, got into his car, and headed to Texas. Coy and Sara were married right away.

The following year, all of Maybelle's and Sara's children came down to Texas, and Maybelle's girls—Helen, June, and Anita—began to sing with the Carters. They were all in grade school. In 1939–1940, they were able to live in San Antonio and go into a local radio station to record a week's worth of songs in one afternoon. Radio, as a medium, reached into every household, from the inner cities to the ravaged, dust-strewn farms of the plains. Shows like the one done by the Carters brought a little respite from the hard years of the Depression. The Carter Family had sung their way into the American cultural landscape.

The next several years were a whirlwind for the Carters. From 1941 to 1943, as the country threw itself into the war effort, the Carter Family worked closer to home in a Charlotte, North Carolina, radio station. By this time, Anita, June, and Helen were thoroughly incorporated into the act. Anita played the standup bass, June the autoharp, and Helen the accordion. June was working on providing comedic moments for the show and was a natural. Sara came from California, where she and Coy were living, because it was good money. When the contract with the Charlotte station expired, that was it. Sara pulled out of the group for good, A.P. seemed disinterested in continuing, and the Carter Family officially disbanded.

Helen, June, Anita, and Maybelle got a job at Richmond's WRNL, a small local station. Now called the Carter Sisters and Mother Maybelle, they were considered a "novelty act." They shared the twice-a-day half-hour program with The Virginia Boys, which took some of the pressure off the girls. June proved to be a natural salesperson and had the personality to go along with the role. She could do the hard sell for any sponsor as well as banter with the WRNL announcer. They didn't make much money on the local station, but they were able to advertise their upcoming appearances. They played in movie theaters, courthouses, schoolhouses, and fire halls throughout Virginia, West Virginia, Pennsylvania, and North Carolina. No trip was too daunting for Maybelle. She had the stamina of a long-distance hauler and drove like one as well. They stayed in boarding houses and flopped with relatives. Once they got to their destination, they'd hook up their own public-address system, tune their instruments, take tickets, and press their handmade clothes with a heated light bulb. "Mama ironed the fire out of everything," said June. "We never went onstage with a wrinkle or uncurled hair. And even though Mama might not have slept for two days, we always looked like we just stepped out of a bandbox."

For the next thirty years, Maybelle Carter would make her life on the road. She was modest and shy of the limelight, but she was enormously talented and the consummate accompanist for her daughters. Her quiet drive and ambition guided the Carter Sisters and Mother Maybelle through the years playing for the Grand Ole Opry in Nashville and then through the resurgence of interest in American folk music in the 1960s. Whenever asked, she would play. She and Sara played together again a couple of times in the 1960s and 1970s, but by that time, Sara's voice was almost ruined due to a lifelong smoking habit. But the cousins who spent their formative musical years together were able to step back in time and pick up where they left off—entertaining audiences with the sweet country songs of their youth.

JUNE CARTER CASH
(1929–2003)
June was the middle daughter. Born to Maybelle and Eck Carter, she was the one Eck always said was his "boy." She was a hard worker, fearless, and funny. June never felt like she had the voice that her sisters, Helen and Anita, had so she developed her comedic side, which catapulted her to prominence at the Grand Ole Opry.

June spent her youth dividing time between schooling and performing. She never thought of herself as a good singer, so she learned to make whatever she was doing funny. Throughout her childhood, she and her sisters performed on radio shows in Virginia and Tennessee as the Carter Sisters and Mother Maybelle. June sparred with announcers and did ads for sponsors. And she and her sisters sang the sweet and sorrowful Appalachian songs in tight, three-part harmony.

In the early sixties, Johnny Cash and June Carter first crossed paths at the Grand Ole Opry, where both were performing. Upon their first meeting, although both were recently married, he said, "Hello, I'm Johnny Cash, and I'm going to marry you someday." "Really?" answered June. "Yeah," said Cash. "Well, good," said June. "I can't wait."

Cash was taking vast quantities of painkillers, amphetamines, and downers. His "I Walk the Line" had been a mega-success, and between 1958 and 1960, he had twenty-five songs on the country-music charts. His drug habit destroyed his first marriage and alienated him from his four daughters, according to Mark Zwonitzer. Yet Cash was somehow able to function, writing songs, recording, and touring.

Johnny Cash booked the Carter Sisters and Mother Maybelle on his roadshow in 1962. Between gigs, he would spend time at Eck and Maybelle's house in Nashville, who told him he could stay there any time he wanted. They had watched Hank Williams self-destruct several years earlier, and they didn't want to see the same thing happen to Johnny Cash. In 1963, Cash recorded "Ring of Fire," written by June and her cousin Merle Kilgore, which may or may not have been about the tortured relationship between Johnny and June.

Johnny Cash. *Source:* Library of Congress.

June was still married to her second husband Edwin "Rip" Nix but was in love with Johnny Cash, according to Zwontizer. However, she would have little to do with him as long as he was abusing drugs.

By 1965, June and Maybelle found themselves going to Johnny's apartment to search for caches of pills he had stashed throughout the place. Cash was on a downward trajectory, and the Carters were trying to save him from himself. Maybelle, Eck, and June didn't shut him out of their lives. But it wasn't until October of 1967 that Johnny Cash hit bottom after he drove a tractor into the lake by his home in an attempt to kill himself. When he didn't die, he told June he wanted to kick his drug habit.

Maybelle, Eck, and June moved into his mansion and took care of him as Cash tried to quit cold turkey. His tortured withdrawal took about a month, and when Johnny came out the other side, June agreed to marry him.

Just months after getting clean, Cash recorded the now-iconic live album at Folsom Prison. A couple of weeks later, he proposed to June Carter onstage in London, Ontario, and within a month they were married, cementing the long collaboration between Johnny Cash and the Carters. In 1971 the variety show *The Johnny Cash Show* began its run on ABC. Johnny, as the host, selected the performers, and the first show featured Bob Dylan, Joni Mitchell, and Doug Kershaw, as well as Johnny and June singing duets accompanied by Maybelle. The show became a smash hit.

June was married three times. The first time was to Carl Smith, a singer, from 1952 to 1956. They had a daughter, Rebecca Carlene Smith, who sang under the name Carlene Carter. Then June married former football player and racecar driver Edwin "Rip" Nix in 1957. Their daughter, Rosie, who was also a country singer, was born in 1958. June and Nix divorced in 1966. The only child of June Carter Cash and Johnny Cash is John Carter Cash, born in 1970.

June Carter Cash won three Grammy Awards, including for Best Traditional Folk Album for *Press On* in 2000. Her last album, *Wildwood Flower*, released after her death in 2003, won a 2004 Grammy Award for Best Traditional Folk Album.

Johnny Cash and June Carter Cash died within months of each other in 2003 after thirty-five years of marriage.

ROSANNE CASH
(B.1955)

Although many of the third-generation Carters have made a mark in the country or country-rock-Americana music industry, Rosanne Cash, Johnny Cash's oldest daughter, with his first wife Vivienne, is the most accomplished. June Carter Cash was Roseanne's stepmother, and June and Rosanne were close.

Rosanne and her three sisters spent the bulk of their childhood in California, and after their parents' separation and subsequent divorce, they saw little of their father while they were children. After Rosanne's graduation from high school, she joined her father's roadshow as a wardrobe assistant and occasional singer. Roseanne lived with Johnny and June when they weren't on the road. In 1974, she sang lead vocal on a version of Kris Kristofferson's "Broken Freedom Song" on Johnny Cash's album *The Junkie and the Juicehead Minus Me*. A couple of years later, her father recorded a song written by Rosanne on his album *One Piece at a Time*.

Fast-forward a dozen years, and Rosanne was married to Rodney Crowell, had children, and lived in Nashville. She had three number-one country records in a row in 1981 and 1982.

It seemed as if Rosanne had everything—assistants, a huge house, a lucrative recording contract, a pile of number-one records, a family—but she was not happy, she admitted in an interview. In 1989 she met producer/songwriter/guitarist John Leventhal, and soon after she and Crowell divorced. Rosanne and Leventhal moved to New York, where they still live.

Throughout the 1990s, Rosanne Cash released five albums, two of which went gold (*Seven Year Ache* and *King's Record Shop*). Her songs were hitting the top of Billboard's country chart with a score of number-one hits, including "My Baby Thinks He's a Train," "Ain't No Money," and "I Don't Know Why You Don't Want Me." During that decade, she had five Grammy nominations.

In 1990, after Cash met Leventhal, she released *Interiors*, a deeply personal album that she produced herself or which she'd written or cowritten all the songs. Although it received a Grammy nomination for Best Contemporary Folk Album, it was the beginning of her break from Nashville and the country music scene. Leventhal and Cash married in 1995.

Over the past two decades, Rosanne Cash has recorded albums, including *Black Cadillac*, released in 2006 after the deaths of her father, stepmother, and mother. *Black Cadillac* landed on a number of top-ten lists that year and was nominated for a Grammy Award. When she toured after the release of the album, it was as part of a multimedia performance with video, narration, and imagery from her family's history. In 2014, Rosanne Cash released *The River & the Thread*, songs written by Cash and her husband Leventhal. This amazing work comes from a trip Cash and Leventhal took through the South, including a visit to her father's childhood home in Dyess, Arkansas. This was the number-one album of 2014 on American radio and was lauded as one of the top albums of the year by a whole host of publications. She and Leventhal won three Grammy Awards for the album.

Rosanne Cash has had her share of medical problems, including brain surgery in 2007 for a rare condition (Chiari I malformation). She wrote about it for the *New York Times* in a piece called "Well, Actually, It *Is* Brain Surgery." Cash has also suffered from polyps on her vocal cords.

In addition to her success in the music industry, Rosanne Cash is a writer of short stories, children's books, essays for publications including the *New York Times* and *Oxford American* magazine, and a *New York Times*-bestselling memoir titled *Composed: A Memoir*. When June Carter Cash died, Rosanne Cash delivered a eulogy in which she said: "[June] was like a spiritual detective: she saw into all your dark corners and deep recesses, saw your potential and your possible future, and the gifts you didn't even know you possessed, and she 'lifted them up' for you to see. She did it for all of us, daily, continuously. . . . She did not give birth to me, but she helped me give birth to my future."

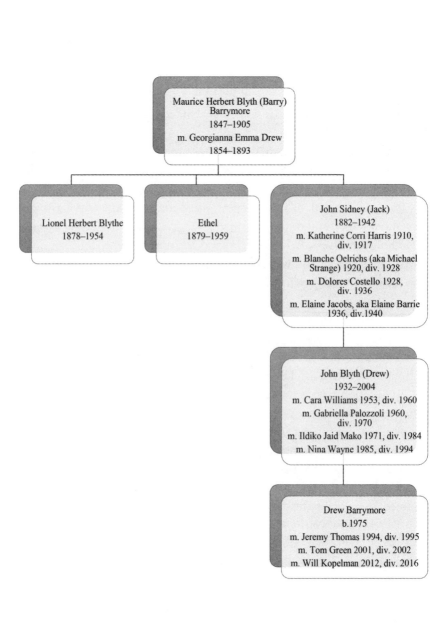

Maurice Herbert Blyth (Barry)
Barrymore
1847–1905
m. Georgianna Emma Drew
1854–1893

Lionel Herbert Blythe
1878–1954

Ethel
1879–1959

John Sidney (Jack)
1882–1942
m. Katherine Corri Harris 1910,
div. 1917
m. Blanche Oelrichs (aka Michael
Strange) 1920, div. 1928
m. Dolores Costello 1928,
div. 1936
m. Elaine Jacobs, aka Elaine Barrie
1936, div.1940

John Blyth (Drew)
1932–2004
m. Cara Williams 1953, div. 1960
m. Gabriella Palozzoli 1960,
div. 1970
m. Ildiko Jaid Mako 1971, div. 1984
m. Nina Wayne 1985, div. 1994

Drew Barrymore
b.1975
m. Jeremy Thomas 1994, div. 1995
m. Tom Green 2001, div. 2002
m. Will Kopelman 2012, div. 2016

14

Barrymore

All the World's a Stage

[Your father] must never know that his youngest child by my lamented sister has ventured upon the stage, for it would be the end of that good man, and the end of many things, I fear.
— Aunt Amelia to Herbert Blythe

The Barrymores have occupied the center stage in American theater and film since the nineteenth century. A family marked by creativity, eccentricity, and its share of tragedy, the "First Family" of theater and Hollywood has been idolized by generations of Americans.

Herbert Arthur Chamberlayne Blythe (Stage Name Maurice "Barry" Barrymore)

According to daughter Ethel, her father, Barry Barrymore, was "born in the dungeons of Fort Agra during the Mutiny." His parents lived in India. His mother died giving birth to him. He was the youngest of seven children. The boy—known as Herbert Blythe then—was raised by his Aunt Amelia in Amritsar, while his father continued with his surveying work. His father then contacted his sister in England, and when Herbert was eleven, he headed off to another aunt, in Harrow, where he excelled at school and fisticuffs. Herbert continued his education at Lincoln College at Oxford and, in addition to his studies, became the amateur boxing champion. His family wanted him to become a barrister, but Herbert wanted to be on the stage. While he was deciding what to do, he won the amateur middleweight boxing championship of England.

When he was in his early twenties, Herbert headed out on the road with his friend comedian Charley Vanderhoff and began playing minor characters on the stage. His family did not approve. His Aunt Amelia wrote, "[Your father] must never know that his youngest child by my lamented sister has ventured upon the stage, for it would be the end of that good man, and the end of many things, I fear." Herbert changed his name to lessen the embarrassment to his family. He found his new last name—Barrymore—from an old playbill and chose the new first name Maurice because he thought it classy. His friends began calling him "Barry."

A young Maurice Barrymore.
Source: Library of Congress.

In 1875, Barry arrived in Boston. He had money from his Aunt Amelia in England. He landed minor parts at first. A critic in the *Boston Evening Transcript* wrote, "[Barrymore's] broad shoulders, manly stride, clean-cut features, handsome teeth, gentlemanly bearing and refined self-possession" would cause him to be a hit among the ladies. He soon found his way to Broadway, where Augustin Daly of the Daly's Fifth Avenue Theatre, offered Barry $75 per week to act. Daly hoped Barrymore would become a stage idol, packing the matinees with women. He would, and he did.

Young Georgianna Emma Drew, known as Georgie, from a famous American acting family, was cast opposite Barry in the Broadway show *Pique.* They became a couple onstage and off. Barrymore was now king of the matinee with "actresses, matinee girls, working women, even charwomen, agreeing that no handsomer man had ever tread the boards of Broadway." Theaters that sold his photographs could not keep them in stock as women put his picture in their lockets, in scrapbooks, and in diaries.

The Fifth Avenue Theatre closed, but Barry went on the road with the touring company. Soon, he and a friend started their own touring company, which included Georgianna's father and many of her family friends.

They were getting good reviews, but many of the cast members were getting ill from the grueling schedule. The business manager later absconded with the company's money. The touring company split into two groups—one going west and the other, including Barry, heading south. Georgie, who was now married to Barry, stayed home because she was pregnant.

The night after Barry's group played in the Opera House in Marshall, Texas, Barry and a couple from the troupe—Ellen Cummins and Ben Porter—headed into the Station Hotel near the railway station and found trouble. Jim Curry, an employee of the railroad and deputy sheriff, began making offensive comments about Cummins. Barrymore told him to stop. According to Barrymore's son, Jack, the following was related to him years later:

"I can do any of you up," said Curry.

"I suppose you could," answered Barrymore, "with your pistol or knife."

"I haven't got any pistol or knife. I'll do it with my bunch of fives," said Curry, as he proudly displayed a fist like a sledgehammer.

"Then," said Barrymore, throwing off his coat. "I'll have a go at you."

But Curry did have a gun, and he shot Barrymore, wounding him in the shoulder. When Porter rushed to Barrymore's aid, Curry shot him. Porter died almost immediately, on the station platform.

The troupe stayed in Marshall until Barry could travel. The doctor who cut the ball out, which had lodged in Barry's back, showed it to him; Barry took it and supposedly said, "I'll give it to my son Lionel to cut his teeth on." Lionel later said that the story could have been true since he was about one at the time. Curry was never convicted, although Barry traveled to Marshall twice to testify. Barry heard later that Curry was killed in a barroom brawl.

Neither Barry nor Georgie were good with money—they either had it, or they didn't. When Barry was recovering from his gunshot wound, he polished his new play, *The Debt of Honor*, a translation of a French drama. Barry wanted to become a playwright. Unfortunately, another play based on the same source opened in New York before Barry got his to the stage, but that didn't stop him from continuing to write plays.

Georgie Drew Barrymore, gifted actor and wife of Maurice Barrymore. *Source:* Library of Congress.

Barry toured in *The Rivals* with his mother-in-law, while Georgie committed to traveling with another play because they needed the money. At this point, they had two children, Lionel and Ethel.

Barry heard that a theater in London wanted to produce *The Debt of Honor,* so he traveled back to England to supervise revisions, afraid that the director would ruin his play. He hadn't been in England for a dozen years but quickly fell back into bachelor life. While there, he met Madame Helena Modjeska, who would play a role in Barry's and Georgie's lives later.

Now with three kids—Lionel, Ethel, and John "Jack"—Barry and Georgie went back on the road while the children stayed with Georgie's mother, Louisa Drew, whom the children called Mummum. She provided much-needed stability to the children of the glamorous stage actors. In Carol Stein Hoffman's biography of the Barrymores, she writes: "Though the children had a great affection for these transient people and their beauty and poise, they never really knew them as they did Mummum.

As adults, they would be reduced to quoting stories they had heard from other people because they were left with so few actual memories themselves of their parents."

The Barrymores knew everyone, and when the children were with them, the children met famous people ranging from Mark Twain and Buffalo Bill to Oscar Wilde. During a dinner at a New York restaurant with Barry, Barry's press agent, and Buffalo Bill, young Jack could hardly stifle his laughter because Cody's hair was so long. Barry saw what was going on and took Jack into the washroom. He told Jack to be careful because William Cody could carve his heart out. Jack was somber for the rest of the meal.

During the 1880s, Barry wrote several plays, including one that was closest to his heart, *Najezda*. *Najezda* was first performed in San Francisco with Madame Modjeska in the leading role. Modjeska played the same part when the play came east, only this time the playwright, Maurice Barrymore, played opposite her. In 1886, Barry took the play to London and brought the whole family with him. They stayed for two years while Barry and Madame Modjeska played their leading roles. At some point, Georgie realized that Modjeska was interested in more than playacting with her husband.

While they were in London, Barry and Georgie attended an elegant dinner party at the Grand Café Royale. In attendance were actress Emily Rigl, bon vivant Oscar Wilde, actress Sarah Bernhardt, Bernhardt's manager, and actress Lillie Langtree. Bernhardt was a leading light of the theater at the time, and she and Barry bantered back and forth all evening. The next day, Georgie sent Bernhardt the French translation of *Najezda*, hoping she would play the lead in a Parisian production. For two years, she held onto the script and then returned it with no comment.

At this same time, *La Tosca*, written by Victorien Sardou with Bernhardt as the lead, premiered in Paris. "It was Maurice's play," wrote Lionel. "There was no question about it. It was an open-and-shut case of plagiarism." Bernhardt dismissed the claim and supposedly said, "If a great man gets the germ of an idea from some—some obscure American, what does it matter? These things often happen." Barry's retort was recorded as: "A man is no less a thief who steals from his own hat rack my walking stick, where I have confidently placed it, and builds an umbrella on it." Later, Puccini wrote the music for *La Tosca* using Sardou's plot, which rankled Lionel Barrymore. "Still, whenever I hear *La Tosca* played, I experience venal emotions."

Barry loved animals and maintained an eclectic collection of creatures throughout his life. There were dogs—lots of dogs—but there were also monkeys, skunks, birds, a bear cub (given to a zoo), beavers, a mongoose, rabbits, cats, and a raccoon. Amy Leslie, the drama critic for the *Chicago News*, wrote, "He is a rather irrational and eccentric lover of animals."

When he and Georgie were on the road, Barry brought as many of his pets as he could, arriving at the train station with wire cages balanced on the back of the car. It got out of hand on a tour for the play *Aristocracy*. When they arrived in San Francisco, the hotel allowed Barry to room with his dog Belle and the two skunks, but when he bought some rare dogs from Japan while he was in the city and wanted to board them as well, he was kicked out of his room. Soon the touring company wasn't even allowed on the train because of the menagerie. Eventually, the tour manager of *Aristocracy* booked a series of one-night stands, and Barry had to quit the show because he found it impossible to travel with eleven dogs, two skunks, various rodents, and at least thirty-five red-headed Japanese birds.

In 1889 the Barrymores moved to an apartment in New York City. Lionel was eleven, Ethel was ten, and Jack was seven. Barry bought a ramshackle farm on Long Island and kept his pets there, and the tenant looked after them. He kept his Clydesdale terrier, Belle of Clyde, with him at all times, including on stage where she lay quietly at his feet. When Belle died, Barry went on a two-day drinking binge.

Georgie became ill on tour in *Wilkinson's Widows* and was given orders to rest. She sailed to the Bahamas to convalesce. While she was gone, the boys stayed at the old farm and had the run of the place with the thirty dogs. When Louisa Drew "Mummum" heard about this, she sent for young Jack. When Georgie came back still ill, she was advised to go west for her health. Thirteen-year-old Ethel went with her. They traveled by ship down to Panama, which they crossed by train, and then headed up the West Coast by ship before finally settling in a little cottage in Santa Barbara, California. It was clear to Ethel that her mother's health was deteriorating. It was 1893, and Georgie was thirty-five when she died. Ethel had to handle all the arrangements and accompany her mother's body back to the East Coast.

When Ethel got to New York, she and the boys went to boarding schools while Barry gave away all their mother's possessions and moved into the Lamb's Club in New York. Within a year, he married Mamie Floyd, who was twenty-five years his junior.

Maurice Barrymore starred in *Becky Sharp*, based on William Thackeray's novel *Vanity Fair*, in 1899. This play was Barry's last Broadway success. He was beginning to forget his lines and was clearly slowing down. After *Becky Sharp*, he acted in vaudeville. In 1901, while Barry was performing at the Lion Palace Theatre in New York, he departed from the script and began ranting on the stage. The *Chicago Tribune*, March 30, 1901, reported: "Maurice Barrymore, the actor, was taken to the pavilion for the insane at Bellevue Hospital and committed for treatment by his son." On April 2, 1901, the *New York Times* reported that "Maurice Barrymore will be removed to Rivercrest Sanitarium; Astoria, L.I. this morning from Bellevue Hospital. That is the decision arrived at by Dr. Newton ... the actor's physician, and Dr. Wildman, the Bellevue insanity expert after an examination of the patient yesterday afternoon. At the conclusion of the consultation, Dr. Newton said that Barrymore was able to talk coherently for several minutes. He would then lapse and would talk irrationally for some time. He said that the actor was a victim of paresis." It was later revealed that he was suffering from tertiary syphilis, according to James Kotsilibas-Davis.

Maurice spent the last four years of his life in a sanatorium. He died on March 25, 1905. Although he had been bedridden for two years prior to his death, his final collapse was sudden, and none of his children were by his side when he died.

LIONEL HERBERT BLYTHE BARRYMORE (1878–1959), ETHEL MAE BARRYMORE (1879–1959), JOHN "JACK" SIDNEY BARRYMORE (1882–1942)

The children of Georgiana Drew Barrymore and Maurice Herbert Blyth Barrymore all became actors, although that was not the first choice of either Lionel or Jack, both of whom wanted to be artists. Lionel Herbert

Blythe Barrymore (1878–1954) left school at fifteen, and his grandmother, the actress Louisa Drew "Mummum," insisted he get a job. So he went on tour with her. He did chores, and in 1893 he appeared on stage in *The Road to Ruin*. Lionel went unnoticed. His grandmother then gave him a bigger role in the Sheridan play *The Rivals*. After the first performance, Drew told Lionel that she made a mistake casting him in the part, which called for an older actor. Moving forward, they were going to cut this scene from the play. Lionel then told his grandmother that he was happy to paint scenery.

Until he was twenty, Lionel stayed with the company, performing bit parts and doing odd jobs. Then he attended the Art Students League for

Lionel Barrymore starred in *The Devil's Garden*, a 1920 silent film now lost. *Source:* Library of Congress.

three years, where he showed some promise. (He would produce etchings for the rest of his life.) But life intruded, and he needed money, so he went back into the theater, getting a job with actor and manager McKee Rankin.

Ethel Mae Barrymore (1879–1959) joined Mummum in Montreal when she was fourteen, after her mother died, where she was given the part of Julia in *The Rivals*. When the play closed, both Mummum and Ethel found themselves back in New York and out of work. Ethel appealed to her uncle Jack Drew, who at that time was Broadway's leading actor and was under contract to the influential manager Charles Frohman. Frohman hired Ethel as a favor to Jack Drew. Three years after doing bit parts, she stepped into the lead role of *The Bauble Shop* when the scheduled actress couldn't go on. Ethel's performance caught Frohman's eye.

Ethel went on tour with the company, playing the part of a maid in *Rosemary*, when she received a telegram from Frohman while they were in St. Louis. He asked if she would like to go to England to play opposite William Gillette in the play *Secret Service*. Gillette was a matinee idol at the time, and Ethel had a crush on him. And she yearned to return to England, which had represented the happiest years of her young life when she lived there for two years as a child.

She was the toast of London. The Prince of Wales caught her first performance as the ingénue and according to Ethel said, "I liked you so much better than the present girl." Ethel "fled, very happy and blushing from head to toe." Ethel stayed in England after the run of *Secret Service*, until she got word that her grandmother was dying. She got on the first ship back to the States.

A young Ethel Barrymore. *Source:* Library of Congress.

John "Jack" Sidney Barrymore (1882–1942) was fifteen when Mummum died. He had spent much of his time with Mummum since he was a little boy and was her favorite grandchild. When her health took a turn for the worse, she and Jack traveled to Larchmont, New York, and rented rooms in a boardinghouse by the sea. Jack acted as a companion and errand boy. During the day, he sketched seascapes while his grandmother talked about the stage. At age seventy-seven, Louisa Drew had seen her children become successful actors, and now her grandchildren were beginning to make their mark. Upon Mummum's death, Lionel wrote that their link to stability and security had disappeared. Mummum's home was the only one they had really known. "This was harder on Jack than on Ethel and me," he wrote. "Jack had been Mummum's favorite, had lived with her and depended upon her. My mother and father, affectionate and generous persons though they certainly were, were actor and actress on the stage, traveling, living in hotels, spending money when they had it, mockingly enduring near-poverty when they didn't. The rearing of offspring was not their forte."

Jack was expelled from Georgetown Preparatory School in November of that year for drinking. In a rare fatherly act, Barry took Jack back to England after Mummum's death, where he and Mamie were on the vaudeville circuit. When Barry and Mamie's run ended, they left Jack in the care of Ethel. When Ethel left London, she gave money to a friend to dole out in small amounts for Jack, who had fallen into the sporting life, much like his father had a generation earlier. Jack made his way back to New York when his money ran out, determined not to join the family business and become an actor.

Jack found a job at the *New York Evening Journal* as an illustrator in the art department, which relieved Ethel. She had just been offered her first big role in Frohman's *Captain Jinks of the Horse Marines*. She had no time to chase after Jack as she studied for her role. Ethel developed opening-night anxiety that would stay with her for the rest of her life. She felt that she would be held responsible for making or breaking the play. The early reviews were terrible, but Ethel was radiant—her long, tiered white dress sprinkled with white silk roses made audiences gasp when she entered the stage. She had arrived.

Ethel Barrymore in her first big role in *Captain Jinks of the Horse Marines*.
Source: Library of Congress.

After being fired from the *Evening Journal* for not turning in his illustrations on time, Jack turned to McKee Rankin, the man who had given Lionel his start and asked for a job. He was not a good actor. One reviewer wrote, "Mr. John Barrymore . . . walked about the stage as if he had been all dressed up and forgotten." Jack maintained he didn't want to be in the theater, writing, "I left the stage to study at art schools, and I only went back to the theater because there is hope—at least money—for the bad actor. The indifferent painter usually starves."

In 1904, Lionel Barrymore wed Doris Rankin, McKee Rankin's daughter. He was twenty, and she was sixteen. They remained married for twenty years. Several years later Ethel Barrymore married Russell Griswold Colt, grandson of the inventor of the Colt revolver, and became a mother in 1909.

Jack moved on from Rankin's management to Charles Frohman's, who represented Ethel, and sent him on tour with *The Dictator*. The star of the play was William Collier, who became a mentor to young Jack. Collier taught Jack about comedic timing and coached him on other aspects of acting. However, Jack's drinking led to missed performances, drunken appearances on stage, and other misbehavior.

The company was waiting in San Francisco for the tour to move on to Australia when the great earthquake of April 17, 1906, hit the city. Jack, who had had a late night of opera (*Carmen* with Caruso and other members of the Metropolitan Opera Company of New York), then supper, had been in bed but minutes when the quake hit. He put on his dress clothes and began walking toward town. "Everywhere whole sides of houses were gone," wrote Jack. "People were hurriedly dressing and, at the same time, trying to gather and throw out what seemed most valuable to them. More prudent persons, who couldn't too readily shake off the habits of shyness nor too quickly forget their decorum, were putting up sheets to shield them from passers-by." He ran into Diamond Jim Brady in front of the Palace Hotel, who was greatly amused to see Jack strolling through the rubble in his evening clothes. When Brady got back to New York, he circulated the story about Jack Barrymore dressing for an earthquake. "Until I talked to Brady it had not occurred to me that I was oddly dressed for the occasion," wrote Barrymore. "I don't know, though, what one should wear at an earthquake."

Jack Barrymore married his first of four wives in 1910. Kathrine Corri Harris was eighteen—a decade younger than Jack. The marriage was fraught from the start, partly because Jack was drinking heavily, which affected both his performances and his marriage. Katherine began going on the road with Jack, taking small parts in the plays in which he was acting. Jack was becoming more interested in comedic roles, and in 1912 he appeared with his sister Ethel in *A Slice of Life* on Broadway. Several more plays and comedies followed that year. He also may have appeared in his first films in 1912. A "Jack Barrymore" is listed as a cast member in four short films made by the Lubin Manufacturing Company in Philadelphia, but they were lost in a fire at the Lubin vaults a couple of years later.

Lionel and Ethel would go on to have successful careers both on the stage and in the movies. Jack, the youngest Barrymore, would have both a tumultuous career and personal life. Over his career, Jack Barrymore would act in dozens of

Jack Barrymore, actor in plays and movies. *Source:* Library of Congress.

plays and movies—he came to prefer movies over plays because he didn't have to play the same part over and over again. Two plays stand out—his portrayals of Shakespeare's *Richard III* (1920) and *Hamlet* (1922–1924). Jack Barrymore, who was very handsome and had a real stage presence, was not known for hewing closely to the script. His ad-libbing (because he couldn't remember his lines) would throw off the other actors, and he often spoke directly to the audience. However, he really embraced the title roles of Richard III and Hamlet, working with vocal coach Margaret Carrington for months to prepare for the roles. His interpretations were inspired, and the critics loved him.

Some of Jack Barrymore's most successful films include *Jekyll and Hyde* (1920), *Beau Brummel* (1924), *The Sea Beast* (1926) (based on the novel *Moby Dick*), *Svengali* (1931), *Grand Hotel* (1932), *Rasputin and the Empress* (1932) (the only sound-era film to star all three Barrymore siblings), *Romeo and Juliet* (1936), *Marie Antoinette* (1938), and his final film, *Playmates* (1941), where he played a broken-down, alcoholic Shakespearean ham named John Barrymore. He also made more than seventy appearances on Rudy Vallee's radio show, *The Sealtest Show*, and was acting on this program when he collapsed for the last time.

Jack Barrymore began drinking as a teenager and never stopped. His drinking affected his performances and his relationships with everyone. His marriage to Katherine Corri Harris ended in divorce in 1917. In 1920 he married Blanche Oelrichs Thomas, better known as the poet Michael Strange, with whom he had a daughter, Diana Blanche Barrymore, in 1921. Barrymore and Strange divorced in 1928. That same year, he married costar Dolores Costello. Their daughter Dolores Ethel Barrymore was born in 1930, and son John Blyth Barrymore (John Barrymore Jr.) was born in 1932. Dolores and Jack divorced in 1935. In 1936, Jack Barrymore married for a final time, to Elaine Jacobs Barrie, who was thirty-four years his junior. They divorced in 1940. He rewrote his will in 1940, leaving virtually everything to his three children and nothing to his ex-wives. That would become academic, because upon the disposition of his property after his death, Barrymore's estate still owed creditors $75,000. John Barrymore was not a model parent. He rarely saw his children, and when he did, he frequently drank to excess. Diana saw him a couple of times when she was a girl and then for a three-week visit when she was eighteen, where she came to despise his drunkenness, according to biographer John Kobler.

By the time of Diana's visit in the late 1930s, Jack Barrymore was in the throes of liver disease, which would kill him a couple of years later. He had collapsed several times during the decade and was hospitalized for enlargement of the liver, Korsakoff's syndrome (memory losses), toxemia, bronchitis, and influenza. He collapsed one last time while rehearsing a scene for *The Sealtest Show* and was taken to the hospital, where he died ten days later from complications resulting from cirrhosis of the liver, hypostatic pneumonia, and kidney failure. He was sixty years old.

JOHN BLYTH "DREW" BARRYMORE
(1932–2004)

Born John Blyth Barrymore, son of Jack Barrymore and Delores Costello, John saw his father only a few times before Jack's death. He was only seventeen when he made his film debut in *The Sundowners* (1950) starring Robert Preston. That same year, Barrymore was the leading man in the Western film *High Lonesome*. He starred in *The Big Night* (1951) and acted with John Derek in *Thunderbirds* the following year. A string of television appearances followed on *Matinee Theatre*, *The 20th Century-Fox Hour*, *Playhouse 90*, and *Schlitz Playhouse*. In the mid-1950s he appeared in several movies, including *While the City Sleeps* (1956), *The Shadow in the Window* (1957), *Never Love a Stranger* (1958), and *High School Confidential* (1958), where he turned in one of his best performances as J. J. Coleridge. He changed his middle name to Drew in 1958.

Like his father, John Barrymore had four wives and had a child with each of them. He married Cara Williams in 1952, and John Barrymore III was born two years later. They divorced in 1958. John moved to Europe after the divorce, where he appeared in about a dozen low-budget films. He met and married film starlet Gabriella Palozzoli in 1960. Two years later, they had a daughter, Blyth. They split in the early sixties and divorced in 1970. Ildiko Jaid Mako and Barrymore married in 1971, and daughter Drew was born in 1975. They divorced in 1985. Finally, John Barrymore and Nina Wayne married that same year and divorced in 1994. They had a child, Jessica Barrymore (1966–2014), who was born out of a relationship they had in the mid-sixties, according to Carol Stein Hoffman.

John Drew Barrymore, father of Drew Barrymore. *Source:* Commons. wikimedia.org.

John Drew Barrymore had repeated brushes with the law. He was sent to jail several times, once for spousal abuse, several times for failing drug tests after car accidents, and a few times for marijuana possession, according to Hoffman. He guest starred on several television shows, including *Gunsmoke, Rawhide,* and *Jericho,* but he received a six-month suspension from SAG (Screen Actors Guild) when he signed on to play a guest role in a *Star Trek* episode and didn't show up. Barrymore spent several years in seclusion and off the grid in a California desert. His final appearances on screen included the film *The Clones* (1974) and an episode of *Kung Fu* that same year.

For most of his later life, he was a recluse. His daughter Drew Barrymore said, "He was the sort of man who had not owned a pair of shoes in 40 years, did not believe in material possessions, and lives the life of a vagabond—often muttering Scripture to passers-by." "I reconciled myself to the fact that he had chosen drugs over being a father. I still love him, but he has never been and never will be a father."

Drew Barrymore (b.1975) has acted in numerous films, including *The Wedding Singer, Poison Ivy, Going the Distance, Never Been Kissed, Ever After, 50 First Dates,* and *Whip It* (which she directed). In 1995 Barrymore and Nancy Juvonen started a film and television production company called Flower Films that has produced almost two dozen films and half a dozen television programs, including *Santa Clarita Diet* (2017–2019), Barrymore's latest on-screen project. A CoverGirl model, fashion icon, actor, director, and producer, Barrymore continues the Barrymore acting dynasty.

Bibliography

The Vanderbilts

"Cornelius Vanderbilt Biography." Biography.com. https://www.biography.com/business-figure/cornelius-vanderbilt, June 15, 2020.

"Harold Vanderbilt, Yachtsman, Is Dead." *New York Times*, July 5, 1970.

McFadden, Robert D. "Gloria Vanderbilt Dies at 95; Built a Fashion Empire." *New York Times*, June 17, 2019.

Patterson, Jerry E. *The Vanderbilts*. New York: Harry N. Abrams, 1989.

Renehan, Edward J., Jr. *Commodore: The Life of Cornelius Vanderbilt*, reprint ed. New York: Basic Books, 2009.

Robehmed, Natalie. "The Vanderbilts: How American Royalty Lost Their Crown Jewels." *Forbes*, July 14, 2014.

Stasz, Clarice. *The Vanderbilt Women: Dynasty of Wealth, Glamour, and Tragedy*. New York: St. Martins Press, 1991.

Stiles, T. J. *The First Tycoon: The Epic Life of Cornelius Vanderbilt*, reprint ed. New York: Vantage, 2010.

The Rockefellers

Chernow, Ron. *Titan: The Life of John D. Rockefeller, Sr*. New York: Vintage Books, 1998.

Collier, Peter, and David Horowitz. *The Rockefellers: An American Dynasty*. New York: Holt, Rinehart and Winston, 1976.

O'Donnell, Carl. "The Rockefellers: The Legacy of History's Richest Man." *Forbes*, July 11, 2014.

"The Rockefellers." *American Experience*. PBS, 2000.

The Fords

Henry Ford II obituary. *New York Times*, September 30, 1987.

Middletown (1929), authors Robert and Helen Lynd

Watts, Steven. *The People's Tycoon: Henry Ford and the American Century*. New York: Alfred A. Knopf, 2005.

Weymouth, Lally. "Tycoon." *New York Times*, March 5, 1978.

Weymouth, Lally. "Foundation Woes the Saga of Henry Ford II: Part Two." *New York Times*, March 12, 1978.

THE GETTYS

Edwardes, Charlotte. "Balthazar Getty: I'm Finally OK with Being a Getty—I've Bought My First Porsche." *Evening Standard*, July 18, 2016.

Fontevecchia, Agustino. "The Getty Family: A Cautionary Tale of Oil, Adultery, and Death." *Forbes*, April 23, 2015.

Fox, Charles. *Kidnapped: The Tragic Life of J. Paul Getty III*. London: Picador, 2018.

La Ganga, Maria L., and Jocelyn Stewart. "Gordon Getty's Second Family Was an Open Secret." *Los Angeles Times*, August 30, 1999.

Loomis, Carol J. "The War Between the Gettys." *Fortune*, January 21, 1985.

Miller, Russell. *The House of Getty*. London: Bloomsbury Reader, 2011.

Pearson, John. *Painfully Rich: The Outrageous Fortune and Misfortunes of the Heirs of J. Paul Getty*. New York: St. Martin's Press, 1995.

Saxon, Wolfgang. "J. Paul Getty Jr., Philanthropist, Dies at 70." *New York Times*, April 18, 2003.

Scarpa, David. "The Enigma of J. Paul Getty, the One-Time Richest Man in the World." *Vanity Fair*, December 22, 2017.

Silva, Horacio. "Family Ties." *New York Times Magazine*. September 23, 2001.

Walsh, John. "Meet the Gettys!" *Tatler*, September 27, 2016.

Whitman, Alden. "J. Paul Getty Dead at 83; Amassed Billions from Oil." *New York Times*, June 6, 1976.

THE ADAMSES

"Charles Francis Adams: The Aged Statesman Gone to His Rest." *New York Times*, November 21, 1886

Ellis, Joseph J. *Founding Brothers: The Revolutionary Generation*. New York: Knopf Doubleday, 2003.

McCullough, David. *John Adams*. New York: Simon & Schuster, 2001.

Stern, Jeremy. "What's Wrong with HBO's Dramatization of John Adams's Story?" History News Network, October 27, 2008

Traub, James. *John Quincy Adams: Militant Spirit*. New York: Basic Books, 2016.

Willis, Matthew. "Who Wrote the Declaration of Independence?" *JSTOR Daily*, July 2, 2016.

THE KENNEDYS

Bzdek, Vincent. *The Kennedy Legacy: Jack, Bobby and Ted and a Family Dream Fulfilled*. New York: Palgrave MacMillan, 2009.

Goodwin, Doris Kearns. *The Fitzgeralds and the Kennedys: An American Saga*. New York: Simon & Schuster, 1987.

Hess, Stephen. *America's Political Dynasties: From Adams to Clinton*. Washington, DC: Brookings Institution Press, 2016.

Klein, Edward. *The Kennedy Curse: Why Tragedy Has Haunted America's First Family for 150 Years*. New York: St. Martin's Press, 2003. www.jfklibrary.org.

THE MORGANS

Chernow, Ron. *The House of Morgan: An American Banking Dynasty and the Rise of Modern Finance.* New York: Grove Press, 2010. Kindle version.

John Pierpont Morgan Jr. obituary. *New York Times,* March 13, 1943.

Strouse, Jean. *Morgan: American Financier.* New York: Random House, 1999.

THE ASTORS

"Astor Family." www.britannica.com/topic/Astor-family, online, revised and updated by Amy Tikkanen, 2011, retrieved September 16, 2020.

Budin, Jeremiah. "The Properties of John Jacob Astor, a Shark among Whales." *Curbed New York,* January 31, 2013.

Irving was also able to interview many of the participants. Called *Astoria: Or, Enterprise Beyond the Rocky Mountains,* it was published in 1836.

Gordon, Meryl. *Mrs. Astor Regrets: The Hidden Betrayals of a Family Beyond Reproach.* Boston: Houghton Mifflin Harcourt, 2008.

Kaplan, Justin. *When the Astors Owned New York: Blue Bloods and Grand Hotels in a Gilded Age.* New York: Viking, 2006.

Kiernan, Frances. *The Last Mrs. Astor: A New York Story.* New York: W.W. Norton & Co., 2007.

Long, Clarence D. *Wages and Earnings in the United States, 1860–1890.* Princeton, NJ: Princeton University Press, 1960. From the National Bureau of Economic Research series.

Stark, Peter. *Astoria: John Jacob Astor and Thomas Jefferson's Lost Pacific Empire.* New York: Ecco, 2015

"William Astor Is Dead." *New York Times,* April, 27, 1892.

THE HEARSTS

"California Gold Rush." History.com. August 29, 2019.

Hearst, William Randolph, Jr., with Jack Casserly. *The Hearsts: Father and Son.* New York: Roberts Rinehart, 1991.

Nasaw, David. *The Chief: The Life of William Randolph Hearst.* Boston: Houghton Mifflin, 2000.

Nasaw, David. "Life at San Simeon." *New Yorker,* March 23, 1998.

Nickliss, Alexandra M. *Phoebe Apperson Hearst: A Life of Power and Politics.* Lincoln: University of Nebraska Press, 2018.

Swanberg, W. A. *Citizen Hearst: A Biography of William Randolph Hearst.* New York: Scribner, 1961.

Thomas, John C. "Why Is Citizen Kane the Best Movie Ever Made?" ReelRundown. https://reelrundown.com/movies/Why-is-Citizen-Kane-the-Best-Movie-Ever-Made. February 12, 2018.

"2016 America's Richest Families Net Worth." *Forbes.com,* June 29, 2016.

William Randolph Hearst obituary. *New York Times,* August 15, 1951, p. 20.

Winkler, John K. "Notes on an American Phenomenon" *New Yorker*, April 30–May 21, 1927.

THE COORS

Baum, Dan. *Citizen Coors: A Grand Family Saga of Business, Politics, and Beer.* New York: William Morrow, 2000.

Byrne, Brendan. "The Rise of the Beer Can." *Atlantic*. May 27, 2016.

Griset, Rich. "Strange Brew." *Coastal Virginia Mag.com*. January 2015.

Jett, Phillip. *The Death of an Heir: Adolph Coors III and the Murder That Rocked an American Brewing Dynasty.* New York: St. Martin's Press, 2017.

Kendall, Justin. "Bill Coors Dies at 102." https://www.brewbound.com/news/bill-coors-dies-at-102, October 15, 2018, retrieved September 16, 2020.

McFadden, Robert D. "William Coors, Brewery Chief and Ultraconservative Voice, Dies at 102." *New York Times*. October 14, 2018.

Roberts, Michael. "The Death of Bill Coors and the Will to Live." https://www.westword.com/news/the-death-of-bill-coors-and-the-will-to-live-documentary-10902379, October 15, 2018, retrieved September 16, 2020.

Saxon, Wolfgang. "Joseph Coors Sr., Beer Maker and Conservative Patron, 85. *New York Times*. March 18, 2003.

THE WYETHS

Duff, James H. *An American Vision: Three Generations of Wyeth Art: N.C. Wyeth, Andrew Wyeth, James Wyeth.* New York: Little Brown & Co., 1987.

Grant, Daniel. "Why Do Critics Still Hate Andrew Wyeth?" *Observer*, August 17, 2016.

Meryman, Richard. *Andrew Wyeth: A Secret Life*, reprint ed. New York: Harper Perennial, 1998.

Michaelis, David. *N.C. Wyeth: A Biography.* New York: Knopf, 1998.

Rawlings, Irene. "Jamie Wyeth: Born to Paint," *Saturday Evening Post*, July 18, 2016.

THE NAMPEYOS

Blair, Mary Ellen, and Laurence Blair. *The Legacy of a Master Potter: Nampeyo and Her Descendants.* Tucson, AZ: Treasure Chest Books 1999.

Fowler, Carol. *Daisy Hooee Nampeyo: The Story of an American Indian.* Minneapolis, MN: Dillon Press, 1978.

Kramer, Barbara. *Nampeyo and Her Pottery.* Albuquerque: University of New Mexico Press, 1996.

THE CARTERS

Cash, Rosanne. "Long Way Home." *Oxford American*. November 24, 2013.

Cash, Rosanne. "Well, Actually, It *Is* Brain Surgery." *New York Times*. April 5, 2008.

Cash, Rosanne. "Rosanne Cash Reflects on What June Carter Was Like as a Stepmother." *Country Living*, August 25, 2017.

Zwonitzer, Mark, with Charles Hirshberg. *Will You Miss Me When I'm Gone? The Carter Family and Their Legacy in American Music.* New York: Simon & Schuster Paperbacks, 2002.

THE BARRYMORES

Barrymore, John. *Confessions of an Actor.* New York: Benjamin Blom, reissued, 1971.

Cohen-Stratyner, Barbara Naomi, ed. *The Drews and the Barrymores: A Dynasty of Actors.* New York: Theatre Library Association, 1988.

Friedlander, Noam. Drew Barrymore Interview. *Telegraph*, August 9, 2010.

Hoffman, Carol Stein. *The Barrymores: Hollywood's First Family.* Lexington: University Press of Kentucky, 2001.

John Drew Barrymore, obituary. *Independent*, December 1, 2004.

Kobler, John. *Damned in Paradise: The Life of John Barrymore.* New York: Atheneum, 1977.

Kotsilibas-Davis, James. *Good Times, Great Times: The Odyssey of Maurice Barrymore.* New York: Doubleday, 1977.

Mundy, Chris. "Drew Barrymore: Wild Thing." *Rolling Stone*, June 15, 1995.

Norden, Martin F. *John Barrymore: A Bio-Bibliography.* Westport, CT: Greenwood Press, 1995.

Index

About the Author

Rachel Dickinson is a writer whose work has appeared in numerous publications including *The Atlantic*, Smithsonian.com, *Outside*, *Men's Journal*, *American Way*, *Aeon*, *Salon*, and *Audubon*. She has been awarded two Travel Classics awards, an American Society of Journalists and Authors award for best book, a National Endowment for the Humanities Youth Fellowship, and a coveted Thomas J. Watson Fellowship. The author of *Falconer on the Edge: A Man, His Birds, and the Vanishing Landscape of the American West*, she lives in Freeville, New York.